Reading & Writing Instruction in the United States: Historical Trends

EDITED BY

H. ALAN ROBINSON

Hofstra University

1977

International Reading Association

ERIC Clearinghouse on Reading & Communication Skills

IRA PUBLICATIONS COMMITTEE 1977-1978 *Chairing,* Harold L. Herber, Syracuse University• Janet R. Binkley, IRA• Faye R. Branca, IRA• Roger Farr, Indiana University• Mary S. Feely, IRA • Lynette Saine Gaines, University of South Alabama • Margaret Keyser Hill, Southern Illinois University • Laura S. Johnson, Morton Grove, Illinois • Lloyd W. Kline, IRA • Connie Mackey, Montreal, Quebec • John McInness, Ontario Institute for Studies in Education, Toronto • John E. Merritt, Open University • Theodore A. Mork, Western Washington State College • Clifford D. Pennock, University of British Columbia • Emma W. Rembert, Florida International University • Robert B. Ruddell, University of California at Berkeley • Cyrus F. Smith, Jr., University of Wisconsin at Milwaukee • Zelda Smith, Gables Academies, Miami • Ralph C. Staiger, IRA• Carl Wallen, Arizona State University• Sam Weintraub, State University of New York at Buffalo.

ERIC/RCS Staff Editor: Kathryn Grossberg

Published September 1977

ERIC Clearinghouse on Reading and Communication Skills
1111 Kenyon Road, Urbana, Illinois 61801

International Reading Association
800 Barksdale Road, Newark, Delaware 19711

Printed in the United States of America

The material in this publication was prepared pursuant to a contract with the National Institute of Education, U.S. Department of Health, Education and Welfare. Contractors undertaking such projects under government sponsorship are encouraged to express freely their judgment in professional and technical matters. Prior to publication, the manuscript was submitted to the International Reading Association for critical review and determination of professional competence. This publication has met such standards. Points of view or opinions, however, do not necessarily represent the official view or opinions of either the International Reading Association or the National Institute of Education.

Library of Congress Cataloging in Publication Data
Main entry under title:

Reading & writing instruction in the United States.

Bibliography: p.
1. Reading—Addresses, essays, lectures.
2. Language arts—Addresses, essays, lectures.
I. Robinson, H. Alan, 1921–
LB1050.R3524   428'.4   77-12428
ISBN 0-87207-855-8

CONTENTS

In memory and in
honor of
Nila Banton Smith,
the historian of the
reading field.

PREFACE

Looking backward seems useful only if the intent is to learn from the past and to profit in the future. The intent of this volume is to provide such an opportunity for teachers, administrators, and researchers. Teachers and administrators, who are often bombarded by diverse materials, dichotomous instructional schemes, and a broad spectrum of educational objectives, by viewing what has happened in the past may then be able to place some limitations on their choices for tomorrow. Researchers, particularly neophyte researchers, may gain some idea of research trends across the years and, perhaps, will be stimulated to generate investigations that appear to be needed. Another purpose of this volume is to encourage historical research designs in the areas of reading and writing. The authors represented here are established scholars, as well as scholars who are in the midst of historical investigations of their own.

The foreword was written by Jonathan Messerli, a noted educational historian and author of *Horace Mann: A Biography*; at this point in his career, he is dean of the School of Education, Fordham University. His succinct statement sets the stage and captures the essence of the book.

Richard E. Hodges, Professor of Education, Director of the School of Education, University of Puget Sound, a national leader in language arts and particularly in spelling, has written a delightful chapter on trends in spelling. As of now, it stands as one of the few integrated discussions of the development of spelling instruction.

Alvina Treut Burrows, Professor Emeritus, New York University, has produced a masterpiece of a chapter on written composition, which probably stands alone as the first written document of its kind to bring together such an effective and cognitive abundance of information about written composition. It's also interesting, in reviewing Dr. Burrows's chapter, to note her continued and valuable contributions to the history of written composition.

Samuel Weintraub, Professor in the Faculty of Educational Studies, State University of New York at Buffalo, is noted for his contributions to reading instruction and research; he is probably best known today for his role as senior author of the annual summaries of investigations relating to reading that appear each year in the *Reading Research Quarterly*. He was the obvious choice to write a chapter about reading research; the chapter he presents here is an interesting and important historical consideration of two strands of research that continue to intrigue investigators.

William P. Cowan is a doctoral candidate at Hofstra University and also is the principal of the Northeast Elementary School, Brentwood, New York. Peter L. Pelosi is a doctoral candidate at the State University of New York at Buffalo. Each of these men has contributed short research summaries which promise to be the frameworks for important contributions once their dissertations are completed.

H. Alan Robinson, Professor of Reading and Director of the Reading/ Communications Resource Center at Hofstra University, wrote a chapter on the history of reading instruction and edited the book. The idea for the volume grew from the activities of the Center at Hofstra University, one of the national dissemination centers cosponsored by the International Reading Association and the ERIC Clearinghouse on Reading and Communication Skills. The Hofstra Center houses and updates the William S. Gray Research Collection in Reading and the Nila Banton Smith Historical Collection in Reading. Thanks are due to Miriam Schleich, Chairperson, Reading Department, Hofstra University, and to John Harvey, Past Dean of Library Service, Hofstra University, for their strong, continuous, enthusiastic support of both the activities of the Reading/Communications Resource Center and the production of this volume.

The editor wishes to thank the International Reading Association and the ERIC Clearinghouse on Reading and Communication Skills for their encouragement of this publication and especially the Publications Committee of IRA for their critical commentary.

H.A.R.

FOREWORD

It has been said, with some justification, that historical ignorance is the mother of "educational innovation." Not heeding Santayana's more general caveat, all too frequently we have sought the chimerical goals of innovation and educational progress, while mindlessly ignoring what we should have learned from the past. As a consequence, our educational endeavors are often misshapen by an arrogance of presentism, tempered only slightly by a recognition of the achievements of other generations.

As narrow educational sectarians of the contemporary, we have refused to concede that others tried many things, learned what was good, and discovered a fair portion of the true. We erroneously have assumed that these discoveries have only appeared in our own times and that only we, through our present ingenuities, have the skills and appropriate ideals with which to come to terms with ignorance, injustice, and greed.

Our preoccupation with the present is intellectually and professionally debilitating on two counts. Perhaps the most obvious of these is that we deny ourselves access to the *products* of human thought and action in dealing with educational problems in other historical settings. Equally important, if less frequently recognized, is that we prevent ourselves from understanding the *processes* by which rational, if fallible, men and women have responded to the educational challenges of their own times.

Thus, by a false claim of self-sufficiency, we have ignored both the products and the processes of the past and thereby have denied subsequent generations access to the benefits to be derived from them.

Many would agree with the criticism that our schools are isolated from the communities of interest that they serve. What is far less frequently recognized is the price our schools pay for their isolation from their own educational history.

Neither those within the profession nor those outside it can be absolved of the blame for this. All too often, those from within have sought change, not necessarily for its own sake but for a legitimization of their professional roles. Frequently this attempt is accompanied by promises of ever greater educational productivity. From the outside, the public has held ever higher and more unrealistic expectations for what our schools can accomplish. These expectations have mushroomed, fed not only by anxieties about the next generation but also by educators' expansive promises, which have little support in our educational history.

For good reason, our undertakings are frequently bedeviled by an endemic instability. Journalists and sentimentalists go slumming in the schools long enough to bemoan the "sad state of education" in their next publications; administrators engage in a survival technique approximating musical chairs; and teachers fall ever more easily into defensive postures protected to a degree by the fragile benefits of collective bargaining. In the best of times, most of us seem to get by; in the worst, we frequently resort to inappropriate responses, running from admission of mea culpa to public scapegoating.

We should also know from history that prolonged neglect can not be rectified by more admonitions. Happily we have begun to do more than this.

As an example, this volume offers the work of a group of scholars examining some of the research trends and some of the ways we have taught reading and writing. In its modest way, it amply demonstrates the virtue of rediscovering that the past is an informative prologue to the present.

JONATHAN MESSERLI

Reading & Writing Instruction in the United States: Historical Trends

In Adam's Fall:
A Brief History of
Spelling Instruction in
the United States

RICHARD E. HODGES
University of Puget Sound

It is possible to spell a word correctly by chance, or because someone prompts you, but you are a scholar only if you spell it correctly because you know how.

Aristotle (340 B.C.)
The Nichomachean Ethics II

The ability to spell correctly has been considered a social virtue throughout the Western world from ancient times to the present. Correct spelling is believed to be important not only for accurate written communication; it is commonly regarded by society to be an attribute of literacy. For these and other reasons, the teaching of spelling has long been an integral part of formal schooling.

Examining past practices in spelling instruction can be a fascinating experience. For, in doing so, we are able to glimpse the daily lives of past generations of school children. More important, however, this backward glance enables us to consider present-day instructional practices in the context of a historical continuum. Santayana (1928—1930), in *The Life of Reason*, warned that "those who cannot remember the past are condemned to repeat it." It is with this admonition in mind that we briefly explore the evolution of spelling instruction in the United States, from early colonial days to the present.

IN THE BEGINNING

Facility with written language was, as it is today, of great importance to the nation's settlers. From the outset of formal education in the U.S., spelling and reading went hand in hand, and the first spellers provided much more than lessons in spelling. These "omnibus" spellers (Nietz 1961) were the depositories of the total curriculum, providing instruction in grammar, handwriting, arithmetic, and religion, as well as in reading and spelling.

Because the early spellers either were shipped directly from England or were reprinted in America, the method of spelling instruction was the same as that practiced in England: the alphabet, or ABC, method, whose origins extended to ancient Greece (Mathews 1966). There was a straightforward purpose underlying the alphabet method, which *The New England Primer* (ca. 1785) made clear:

> He that ne'er learns his A, B, C,
> Forever will a Blockhead be:
> But he that learns these letters fair
> Shall have a Coach to take the Air.

With this method, the pupil first learned the order and names of the large and small letters of the alphabet, a task which occupied some children for many months. Then letter combinations (such as *ab, eb, ib*) were learned, spelled out and pronounced, and this was followed by their use in words made up of increasing numbers of syllables. *The New England Primer*, for example, presented children with the task of mastering 180 syllables, from *ab* to *zu*; eighty-four 1-syllable words, from *age* to *would*; forty-eight 2-syllable words, from *ab-sent* to *mu-sic*; twenty-four 3-syllable words, from *a-bu-sing* to *ho-li-ness*; eighteen 4-syllable words, from *a-bi-li-ty* to *gra-ci-ous-ly*; fourteen 5-syllable words, from *a-bo-mi-na-ble* to *ge-ne-ro-si-ty*; and twelve 6-syllable words, from *a-bo-mi-na-tion* to *qua-li-fi-ca-ti-on*.

Following *The New England Primer*, the most widely used speller of the colonial period was Dilworth's *A New Guide to the English Tongue*, first published in England in 1740 and printed in the colonies seven years later. After mastering the alphabet, pupils were drilled on such words as *Nebuzaradum, Estremadure, Saxigesime, Abelbethmaleah, Aberconiway, Caglian, Clarencester, Compostella, Elezar*, and *Thyatria*. The first wholly American speller was published in 1770, Benezet's *Pennsylvania Spelling Book; or, Youth's Friendly Instructor*, which, however, continued to use both the content and the method of the English texts (Carpenter 1963).

With the colonies' independence from England, indigenous spellers proliferated. The first prolific textbook writer in the United States was Noah Webster, who produced not only a speller but a grammar, a U.S. history, and two dictionaries, as well. Webster's spellers shaped the teaching of spelling for well over a century. Approximately 75 million copies of various revisions of his original text were printed between 1783 and the end of the nineteenth century. Webster's first edition, *Grammatical Institute of the English Language, Part One*, was fashioned after Dilworth, although Webster replaced English place names with U.S. ones, supplanted religious content with Poor Richard's percepts, and changed the British form of syllabication so that the suffixes *ti-on*, *ci-on*, and *si-on* were treated as one syllable. Retitling his speller *The American Spelling Book* in 1787, Webster sold approximately three million copies over the next twenty years (Carpenter 1963; Nietz 1961).

The massive sales of Webster's "blue-backed" speller served, however, to perpetuate archaic methodology and content. To gain spelling ability, Webster asserted, required that the pupil master each step of the alphabet method before moving to the next (Horn 1957). Aware of the tediousness of this approach, Webster suggested that the dull monotony of learning to spell could be relieved by reading lessons. Spelling lessons were not intended, he said, to teach word meaning. Besides, "since understanding cannot keep pace with memory, children could profit from learning to spell and pronounce words not within their capacities because as their capacities grow so would their understanding" (Shoemaker 1936).

Despite the widespread popularity of Webster's speller, it was not without its critics and competitors. Cobb, who published his own *Speller* about 1821 (Nietz 1961), chided Webster for departing from the "principles of orthography and orthoëpy" and for being inconsistent with his own dictionary. Such criticisms probably induced Webster to publish a new dictionary, the *American Dictionary*, in 1828, which was followed a year later by a revised speller, The *Elementary Spelling Book* (Carpenter 1963; Nietz 1961), in which spelling, syllabication, and pronunciation conformed to the 1828 dictionary. U.S. pronunciation and spelling were not, however, universally accepted. A Reverend Cheever (1846) was led to comment that

> innovations should be resisted, nor should any mere Lexicographer nor University, nor knot of Critics, have it in their power to make them prevalent. . . . [The spelling trouble of the time was] owing in great measure to Dr. Webster's unfortunate orthographical eccentricities, which have set so many spellers and journeyman printers agog to imitate him.

The *Elementary Spelling Book* marked a significant change in spelling textbooks, for it placed greater emphasis upon spelling and less emphasis upon reading and grammar. Separate spelling texts began to increase, and one of the first was Cummins's 1819 *Pronouncing Spelling Book* (Nietz 1961), in which children learned to spell such words as *volubility*, *subtilization*, *cicatrization*, *circumlocution*, *prosopopoeia*, and *antimonarchical*.

That the words studied for spelling might also be functional was not an unknown concept, however. Among the first texts to include, according to the author, words frequently used in speaking and writing was Fiske's *The New England Spelling Book* (Nietz 1961), published in 1803, which included this interesting list of words:

axe	bright	Damn	fraud
aught	broad	dawn	fraught
badge	brogue	dead	freight

No better description can be provided of instructional method during the early nineteenth century than the following account (Alcott 1831) of one man's recollection of how he was taught to spell:

> To teach spelling, a lesson was assigned, consisting of a certain number of columns arranged in alphabetical order, as the words of our spelling books usually are, which the pupil was requested to study over and over, until he could recollect and spell them from memory. None of them were ever defined for him; nor was he requested or encouraged to seek for definitions for himself. In this manner, one word suggested, by association, the next; the second, the third; and so on. No faculty was called into exercise but the memory. If a word was misspelled, the next pupil who could spell it was allowed to take his place, or "go above him," as it is called. He who was at the head of the class at evening had a credit mark, and sometimes a written certificate of good scholarship. Indeed, emulation was *the only motive to exertion* which I ever knew employed in the school, except compulsion.

A CHANGE IN APPROACH

Dissatisfaction with this time-honored method of teaching spelling was perhaps most notably articulated by Horace Mann. While secretary of the Massachusetts Board of Education, Mann had visited schools in a number of European countries and had returned from his trip with deep convictions about the superiority of the "whole-word" method over the alphabet method. His views of spelling instruction have served to enlighten us about the purposes of education during the middle part of the nineteenth century and about what he and his followers regarded as the basis of spelling ability.

Mann claimed (1839) that the superior spelling method was one with "power to arrest and fix the attention of the learner," which the alphabet method failed to do. Moreover, the alphabet failed, Mann said (1840), to foster the pupil's mastery of correct pronunciation.

> When a child is taught the three alphabetic sounds *l e g*, and then is told that these three sounds, when combined, make the sound *leg*, he is untaught in the latter case what he was mistaught in the former. *L e g* does not spell *leg*, but if pronounced quickly, it spells *elegy*.

According to Mann (1840), children should be taught to recognize whole words before being taught the letters of which they are composed. Pupils should begin with familiar words which name familiar objects.

> When we wish to give to a child the idea of a new animal, we do not present successively the different parts of it, an eye, an ear, the nose, the mouth, the body, or a leg; but we present the whole animal, as one object.

Mann was especially concerned by the fact that pupils were not required to correct their misspellings and, worse, that teachers commonly corrected the misspelled words for them. The pupil derived "about as much advantage in orthography, from having the teacher spell all his words for him, as he would derive of physical strength, from having the teacher eat all his meals for him" (Mann 1839).

Although he is rightfully credited with introducing emerging European views of childhood into education in the U.S., Mann (1839) did not dismiss the ready use of harsh treatment when necessary. "The laws of nature . . . invariably attach some inconvenience or suffering to error," he observed, and "in stubborn cases, perhaps, some degree of humiliation may be resorted to [in spelling instruction]."

In a very important lecture about the teaching of spelling, Mann (1840) was critical of the general population's lack of spelling ability, the blame for which he placed both on the difficulties inherent in the English writing system and on the manner in which spelling was being taught. He then set forth a rationale for separating spelling from other school subjects, and he urged that separate spellers be prepared "mainly with reference to the ease, pleasure, and progress of the learner, fitted to arouse his curiosity, and adapted to those faculties of his mind which are the most active." Spelling books, he said, therefore should be designed according to three principles: (1) the ease of their use, (2) the pleasure they afforded the pupil, and (3) their ability to foster pupils' progress in orthography, pronunciation, and intelligence.

The learning principle which should be used in teaching spelling was the "law of association," Mann said. Accordingly, all similarly formed words should be presented in a common table, much in the manner of a multiplication table. Thus pupils, by constant drill in spelling these words, would be able, by association, to recall the spelling of all words in the table when they recalled the spelling of any one of the words. The rote memory of words, not the application of spelling rules, Mann claimed, underlay spelling ability. He did suggest, however, that spelling mastery was fostered when several senses were brought into play, when eye, ear, and hand "establish by the power of frequent association, that peculiar sequence of letters which spells each word."

As graded schools proliferated in the mid-nineteenth century, graded textbooks did also, at least to the extent that a distinction was recognized between beginning and advanced materials. One of the first such texts in the area of spelling was Sanders's *The Primary Spelling Book*, published in 1858 and followed a few years later by his *Test-Speller*, which was meant for use in teacher institutions and in the advanced classes of the common school. Sanders's *Test-Speller* contained about five thousand words, including *quadriphylous, pasquinade, metempsychosis, xanthophyll*, and *umquhile* (Nietz 1961).

While spelling instruction continued to be regarded as a means of improving mental discipline, criticism mounted regarding the manner of instruction and the lack of attention given to word meanings. A Reverend Davis (1839) contended that

> the common mode of spelling is to put out words to a class, and when one fails to let the next try, and the next, and so on, until someone spells the word correctly, who takes the place of the one who commenced it, as a reward for his superior skill. . . . [This practice] discourages the poorer scholars in the class, and brings into exercise a spirit of emulation and strife which however harmless it may be in childhood, has, no doubt, an unhappy influence upon the future character. It is the spirit which, among political men, is called party spirit, and among religious men sectarian zeal.

Yet another critic, C. Greene (1851), argued that spelling ability involves analytic, as well as visual and auditory, skills and that verbal memory, upon which the prevalent instructional method depended, was the lowest of intellectual faculties. A knowledge of word meaning, Greene claimed, was required if the pupil's interest in learning how to spell correctly was to be fostered.

The emphasis given to spelling in the nineteenth century went beyond the confines of the classroom. Spelling was a part of the fabric of society itself and found its most popular expression in the spelling bee, or spelldown. The competition of the spelling bee had deep roots in the past, as noted by the following account from Coote's *The Englishe Scholemaster* (Rice 1897), in which two students, John and Robert, are engaged in a spelldown in the year 1596.

Iohn: How write you *Circle*?

Robert: S, i, r, c, l, e.

Iohn: Nay, now you misse: for if you looke in the table, you shall find it *Circle*. Therefore now you must appose me.

Robert: I confesse mine error, therefore I will try if I can requite it: what spelleth b, r, a, n, c, h?

Iohn: Branch.

Robert: Nay, but you should put in *u.*

Iohn: That skilleth not, for both waies be usuall.

Robert: How spell you *might?*

Iohn: M, i, g, h, t.

Robert: Why put you in *gh* for m, i, t, e, spelleth *mite?*

Iohn: Truth, but with *gh* is the truer writing, and it should haue a little sound.

After further opposing, they decide to continue the next day, and John boasts:

> Do your worst, I wil prouide likewise for you, and neuer giue you ouer untill I haue gotten the victorie: for I take not so much pleasure in any thing els all day.

Robert: I am of your mind: for I haue heard our maister say, that this apposing doth very much sharpen our wits, help our memorie, and many other commodities.

The competitiveness of the spelldown appealed to Puritan New Englanders and became a form of entertainment in many communities. Commonly called a "spelling school" in order to give propriety to a social event, spelling bees flourished and then waned in the early nineteenth century as other forms of entertainment became available. But spelling bees continued to flourish along the western frontier, where the "attainment of conventional spelling was seen as a symbol of culture" (A. W. Read 1941). The high regard given good spellers in the nineteenth century is reflected in the following comment made by Mark Twain (1931):

> In the old times people spelled just as they pleased. That was the right idea. You had two chances at a stranger then. You knew a strong man from a weak one by his iron-clad spelling, and his handwriting helped you to verify your verdict. Some people have an idea that correct spelling can be taught, and taught to anybody. That is a mistake. The spelling faculty is born in man, like poetry, music and art. It is a gift; it is a talent. People who have this gift in a high degree need only see a word once in print and it is forever photographed upon their memory. They cannot forget it. People who haven't it must be content to spell more or less like—like thunder—and expect to splinter the dictionary wherever their orthographical lightning happens to strike.

For others, diligence, hard work, and external motivation were deemed necessary, as witnessed by the case of Reverend Arnold, who in 1830 was tried in a New Hampshire court for beating his adopted son, Joseph Pray, for his failure to spell and pronounce a word correctly. Shortly thereafter, a booklet entitled *The Astonishing Affair* was published in which Reverend Arnold was defended for his action because he had "acted conscientiously in inflicting said punishment, and did it out of pure motives" (Carpenter 1967). The belief that spelling ability is either a born talent or the consequence of hard work remains with us and, although the importance of spelling within the curriculum has lessened, its status in the larger society has not.

With the rise of social Darwinism and a growing ferment in the application of science to the solution of educational problems, there emerged on the scene a young pediatrician, Dr. Joseph M. Rice (1897), whose interest in educational reform led him to study the teaching of spelling in some twenty U.S. cities in the early 1890s. Space does not permit a thorough look at Rice's analysis of the spelling achievement of some 33 thousand students. Generally, he observed that the school environment (he contrasted "mechanical" and "progressive" schools) had little effect upon spelling achievement. He further observed that out-of-school variables, such as age, nationality, and home environment, had no substantial effect upon spelling achievement. On the basis of his findings, he concluded that, since the results of spelling instruction were not materially modified by conditions over which the teacher had no control, four factors must lie at the root of students' spelling difficulties.

(1) *Time allotted to spelling:* Since spelling achievement did not improve when words were studied forty to fifty minutes or ten to fifteen minutes each day, more than fifteen minutes spent in spelling study, said Rice, was a waste of time, and he recommended that no more than fifteen minutes a day should be given to spelling instruction.

(2) *Word selection:* In order to make spelling study more efficient, words should be carefully selected and graded as to both orthographical difficulty and relationship to pupils' vocabularies; precedence should be given to common words, particularly those that are frequently misspelled (for example, *to, too, their, hear, does*).

(3) *Teaching method:* Rice found that spelling achievement was little affected by the mode of instruction; for example, whether pupils were taught orally or in writing, whether words were spelled in isolation or in sentences, or whether the words were first studied syllable by syllable. He thus recommended that instruction include many methods and devices.

(4) *Teacher effectiveness:* Having determined that neither method nor time affected spelling achievement, Rice concluded that the teacher's skills must be the key to effective spelling instruction. The effective teacher, said Rice, was one who was acquainted with many methods of instruction and could apply them where appropriate.

THE SCIENTIFIC MOVEMENT

Rice's study was instrumental in shaping the study of spelling method thereafter, and during the early twentieth century scores of researchers began to examine spelling instruction from a variety of vantage points. By 1919, enough evidence had been compiled about spelling method, according to Horn, that it was possible to "gather together existing experimental evidence which throws light on economy in learning to spell and to focus this evidence upon the solution of such problems as confront the classroom teacher." Citing 133 sources, Horn (1919) prepared a list of forty-one principles of spelling method and concluded that

> efficiency in teaching spelling is to be increased by a specific attack on the individual words to be learned. This is in line with the whole tendency in modern experimental education, a tendency which has been well outlined by Thorndike in his discussion of education as the formation of specific bonds. In harmony with this point of view the problem of spelling has been attacked. First, by seeking to discover precisely the words which we most frequently need to spell; second by attempting to grade these words scientifically; third by attempting to discover the most economical methods of learning them; and fourth by devising means by which progress in learning the words may be measured.

A sampling of Horn's forty-one principles:

> Developing pride in spelling is not a substitute for drill in spelling.

> The first step in economy of time in learning to spell is to see to it that the pupil learns to spell those words which he needs to spell and no others.

> Those words which are commonly used by the children in any given grade should be placed in that grade.

> If spelling is to be taught daily, the spelling periods should not be more than fifteen minutes in length.

> Grouping words is of doubtful value, except for immediate recall.

> The emphasis in presenting the word should be on visual imagery.

> The correct pronunciation of a word is a very important factor in learning to spell it.

> It is important to expend some time on drill in recalling the

visual image of the word rather than to expend all the time in impressing this image.

The amount of repetition necessary for fixing a word varies greatly with individuals.

The efficiency of drill in a given spelling period is increased by distributing the drill on a given word so that practice on other words intervenes.

It is important that each pupil be taught how to learn to spell.

The steps Horn set forth for word study were:

(1) The first step in learning to spell a word is to pronounce it correctly. If you do not know how to pronounce a word, look up the pronunciation in the dictionary. When you are certain that you know how the word is pronounced, pronounce it, enunciating each syllable distinctly and looking closely at each syllable as you say it.

(2) Close your eyes and try to recall how the word looks, syllable by syllable, as you pronounce it in a whisper. In pronouncing the word be sure to enunciate the syllables carefully.

(3) Open your eyes to make sure that you were able to recall the correct spelling.

(4) Look at the word again, enunciating the syllables distinctly.

(5) Recall again, with closed eyes, how the word looked.

(6) Check again with the correct form. This recall (as in 2 and 5) should be repeated at least three times, and oftener if you have difficulty in recalling the correct form of the word.

(7) When you feel sure that you have learned the word, write it without looking at the book, and then check with the correct form.

(8) Repeat this two or more times without looking either at the book or at your previous attempts.

(9) If you miss the word on either of these trials, you should copy it in your spelling notebook, since it probably is especially difficult for you.

Horn's set of principles of spelling method are demonstrative of the impact that the scientific movement in education had had upon the spelling program. Particularly significant was the notion that the utility of a word should be the basis for its place in the spelling program. As noted by Pryor (1919),

the function of spelling is to teach children how to spell and use in an accurate way the words which are commonly met with in life and to form such habits of study that new words will be learned as the need for them arises.

According to Breed (1925), five sources were available from which to derive a functional spelling vocabulary: adult written discourse, children's written discourse, adult written correspondence, children's misspellings, and, most promising of all, a combination of children's written work and adult correspondence. A number of studies were undertaken through the years to identify those words most needed for communication (Anderson 1921; Buckingham and Dolch 1936; Fitzgerald 1951; Gates 1937; H. Greene 1954; Horn 1926; Rinsland 1945). Identifying the optimal list of words for study and agreeing where they should be placed in the spelling program were, however, two different matters, as Selke's (1929) analysis of the vocabulary presented in ten spellers showed. Selke determined that the ten spellers contained a total of 8427 different words, of which only 1080 (thirteen percent) were common to all the texts, and further, that only three words—*appreciate* (grade seven), *doll* and *ice* (grade two)—had the same grade placement in the ten texts.

EMPHASIS ON THE LEARNER

A school superintendent in Chelsea, Massachusetts, B. C. Gregory (1907—1908), deplored the lack of attention then being given to the implications of child study for developing the spelling curriculum. Citing Froebel, Gregory urged that pupils be made conscious of their potential for learning and not of their failures. If one looked at children's spelling errors, Gregory claimed, one could see that "it is our spelling that is irrational, and it is the bad speller that is rational."

Twenty years later, Sudweeks (1927) concluded that learning to spell was a multisensory activity:

> The science of biology (or of its derivative, psychology) supplies the basis of spelling method. Children learn to spell by seeing the letters of a given word or by hearing their sounds and by writing and speaking the letters in the order in which they are seen and heard. Seeing and hearing are forms of "impression"; writing and speaking are forms of "expression." These two form the bases for four kinds of images: (1) the sight of a word, (2) the sound of a word, (3) the way it "feels" when written, and (4) the way it "feels" when spoken.

A half dozen years later, Almack and Staffelbach (1933), in a review of the spelling research literature, concluded that psychology provided the most important insights into spelling method and that psychologists had shown experience to be the basis of learning and thus the proper basis of instruction. They criticized the prevalent practice of a pretest on Monday, word study on Tuesday, retesting and a review on Wednesday, individual study on Thursday, and a final test on Friday, acknowledging that the plan was systematic enough but arguing that it simply did not promote learning. This plan, they pointed out, was based on the fallacious assumption that units of study are of equal difficulty and thus demand the same time distribution and pupil effort, week in and week out. The plan, in short, was aimed at group instruction to the detriment of the individual. School work, they said, should be meaningful to *individual* children, and the best spelling method was one that appealed to the practical nature of the child, by varying procedures, limiting study to commonly used words, promoting mastery through rivalry with one's own record, and using words in "real-life" situations, such as classroom projects.

Despite the progressive spirit that flourished through the 1930s and 1940s, spelling instruction actually did not stray far from the course charted by such educational researchers as Ernest Horn. Nearly thirty years after his formulation of the forty-one principles (1919), Horn once again summarized research evidence on spelling method and concluded that the available evidence served mainly to reinforce the assertions that the content of spelling instruction should include only the words most frequently needed in adult and child writing and that learning to spell rested essentially upon visual memory (Horn 1938).

Spelling instruction by mid-twentieth century looked dramatically different from its ancestor of one hundred years earlier. Yet, while views of the learner and of the purposes of instruction had changed, the view that the English orthography was irrational had not. The emphasis upon the utility of the spelling vocabulary rested, after all, upon an assumption that, since one could not depend upon orthographic rules to guide the act of spelling, the rote memory of the words needed in writing was the most efficient learning process.

INFLUENCE OF LINGUISTICS

Then, in the early 1950s, another branch of scientific inquiry, linguistics, emerged as a possible source for the improvement of the spelling program. A few linguists, notably Bloomfield (1933), asserted that English orthography was not the irrational graphic tool it was said to be but that it contained principles whose systematic presentation could benefit the pupil setting about to master the written code. Among the first education-directed studies to examine the validity of this premise was that conducted by Hanna and Moore (1953). Examining a composite of the three thousand words most commonly found in the spelling texts of the period, they observed the existence of relationships between speech sounds and written words which, they concluded, could benefit the learner. They made several recommendations. (1) Some time should be spent daily on "the business of learning to translate sounds into written symbols." (2) Spelling instruction should be integrated with other curricular subjects in order to emphasize the meaning and current usage of words. (3) Pupils should discover inductively the spelling patterns in their study words. (4) Spelling instruction should be sequenced so that pupils study simple and powerful spelling patterns before studying more complex patterns. (5) The few irregular words needed for written communication should be, and need to be, individually memorized.

The emphasis upon induction as the mode of learning to spell could, of course, only be made if there was reason to believe that there were reliable spelling patterns, or "rules," inherent in the orthography. While the Hanna-Moore study was not universally well received throughout the educational community, it served to focus an emerging branch of scientific inquiry upon the perennial controversy over the usefulness of phonics in spelling instruction.

In a critique of the Hanna-Moore study, Horn (1957) attempted to place in context the possible utility of phonic knowledge in the spelling program. Horn strongly disagreed with the claim by Hanna and Moore that "pupils can arrive deductively [Horn's term] at the spelling of most words they can pronounce." The English orthography was not as systematic as they claimed, he maintained, pointing out that philologists, phoneticians, and lexicographers have perennially urged its reform. Although some spelling rules might be useful, they needed to be viewed in the context of the law of association and in terms of negative and positive transfer. In short, Horn argued, the proof of a rational orthography was, by no means, all in.

By the early 1960s, the application of linguistic science to the study of written language and its teaching had, however, taken a firm hold. Hanna and others, using computer technology, conducted an intensive investigation of spelling patterns in over seventeen thousand words (Hanna, Hanna, Hodges, and Rudorf 1966; Hodges 1966). Venezky (1967) reported on his study of the letter-to-sound patterns in approximately twenty thousand words. By the end of the decade, it had become commonplace to find articles in most educational journals which had as their basis the application of linguistic principles to the teaching of spelling and reading.

While the conventional wisdom about the nature of spelling and its teaching is not easily altered (see, for example, Sherwin's extensive review of spelling research, 1969), the 1970s herald a new and significant attempt to bring to bear upon the subject contemporary views of learning and language. Indicative of efforts to relate linguistic and psychological theory to spelling instruction is the work of the Simons (1973), who pointed out that the crucial question is not whether phonemic information is useful in learning to spell but how it can most effectively be introduced and how it is best used by the speller.

Recalling Gregory's (1907–1908) observation, mentioned earlier, that the implications of child study had great significance for the spelling program, the present decade is marked by a growing number of researchers who are enhancing our understanding of how children acquire language and how their linguistic knowledge functions in the development of their written language skills (Chomsky 1970; Fisher 1973; Frost 1973; C. Read 1975).

CONCLUSION

Over three hundred years have elapsed since the first spelling lesson was taught in what is now the U.S. We have seen that the major issues underlying the teaching of this subject center on the source of spelling ability, the nature of the English orthography, and the methods of instruction which follow from assumptions held about them. Current content and method are amalgams of old and new, reflecting the evolution of spelling as a school subject. Such polar issues as the place of rote drill and the understanding of rules in spelling instruction remain for scholar and layperson alike. Santayana's observation quoted at the outset of this review provides a fitting closing reminder. As we look ahead in our efforts to improve the outcomes of spelling instruction, we must not forget to look back, as well, for hindsight can help us to avoid repeating many questionable practices carried on in the name of good intention.

REFERENCES

Alcott, William A. "History of a Common School from 1801 to 1831." *American Annals of Education* 1 (November 1831): 509.

Almack, John C., and Staffelbach, E. H. "Method in Teaching Spelling." *The Elementary School Journal* 34 (November 1933): 175—85.

Anderson, W. N. "Determination of a Spelling Vocabulary Based upon Written Correspondence." *University of Iowa Studies in Education* 1 (1921): 1—66.

Bloomfield, Leonard. *Language.* New York: Henry Holt and Co., 1933.

Breed, Frederick S. "What Words Should Children Be Taught to Spell?" *The Elementary School Journal* 26 (October, November, December 1925): 118—31, 202—14, 292—306.

Buckingham, B. R., and Dolch, E. W. *A Combined Word List.* Boston: Ginn and Co., 1936.

Carpenter, Charles. *History of American Schoolbooks.* Philadelphia: University of Pennsylvania Press, 1963. Pp. 148—59.

Cheever, George B. *Wanderings of a Pilgrim.* New York: John Wiley, 1846. Pp. 49—50.

Chomsky, Carol. "Reading, Writing, and Phonology." *Harvard Educational Review* 40 (1970): 287—309.

Clemens, Samuel Langhorne [Mark Twain]. Reported in the *St. Louis Republican,* 23 May 1875. Reprinted in *Missouri Historical Review* 25 (April 1931): 532—33.

Criscoe, Betty L. "A Historical Analysis of Spelling Instruction in the United States 1644—1973." Doctoral dissertation, Syracuse University, August 1973.

Davis, Emerson. "The Teacher Taught; or, The Principles and Modes of Teaching." *The Common School Journal* 1 (1839): 26—29.

Fisher, Eugenia. "A Linguistic Investigation of First Grade Children's Spelling Errors as They Occur in Their Written Compositions." Doctoral dissertation, University of Virginia, 1973. [ED 086 974]

Fitzgerald, James A. *A Basic Life Spelling Vocabulary.* Milwaukee: Bruce Publishing Co., 1951.

Frost, James A. "Development of Competence in Spelling: A Linguistic Analysis." Doctoral dissertation, Case Western Reserve University, 1973. [ED 085 706]

Gates, Arthur I. *A List of Spelling Difficulties in 3876 Common Words.* New York: Bureau of Publications, Teachers College, Columbia University, 1937.

Greene, Christopher A. "Methods of Teaching Spelling." In *The Lectures Delivered before the American Institute of Education.* Boston: Ticknor, Reed, and Fields, 1851.

Greene, Harry A. *The New Iowa Spelling Scale.* Iowa City: State University of Iowa, 1954.

Gregory, B. C. "The Rationale of Spelling." *The Elementary School Teacher* 8 (1907—1908): 40—55.

Hanna, Jean S., and Hanna, Paul K. "Spelling as a School Subject: A Brief History," *The National Elementary Principal* 38 (May 1959): 8—23.

Hanna, Paul R.; Hanna, Jean S.; Hodges, Richard E.; and Rudorf, Erwin H. *Phoneme-Grapheme Correspondences as Cues to Spelling Improvement.* Washington, D.C.: U.S. Government Printing Office, U.S. Office of Education, 1966. [ED 003 321]

Hanna, Paul R.; Hanna, Jean S.; and Hodges, Richard E. *Spelling: Structure and Strategies.* Boston: Houghton-Mifflin Co., 1971. [ED 050 102]

Hanna, Paul R., and Moore, James T., Jr. "Spelling: From Spoken Word to Written Svmbol." *The Elementary School Journal* 53 (February 1953): 329—37.

Hodges, Richard E. "A Short History of Spelling Reform in the United States." *Phi Delta Kappan* 45 (1964): 330—32.

———. "The Case for Teaching Sound-to-Letter Correspondences in Spelling." *The Elementary School Journal* 66 (March 1966): 327—36.

Horn, Ernest. "Principles of Method in Teaching Spelling, as Derived from Scientific Investigation." In *Fourth Report of the Committee on Economy of Time in Education,* edited by G. M. Whipple, pp. 52—77. Bloomington, Illinois: Public School Publishing Co., 1919.

———. *A Basic Writing Vocabulary.* University of Iowa Monographs in Education. Iowa City: University of Iowa, 1926.

———. "Contributions of Research to Special Methods: Spelling." In *The Scientific Movement in Education,* pp. 107—114. Chicago: University of Chicago Press, 1938.

———. "Phonetics and Spelling." *The Elementary School Journal* 57 (May 1957): 424—32.

Mann, Horace. "Spelling." *The Common School Journal* 1 (1839): 354—57.

———. "Lecture on the Best Mode of Preparing and Using Spelling Books." In *Lecture on Education.* Boston: Marsh, Copen, Lyon, and Webb, 1840.

Mathews, Mitford M. *Teaching to Read: Historically Considered.* Chicago: University of Chicago Press, 1966. [ED 117 649]

Nietz, John. *Old Textbooks.* Pittsburgh: University of Pittsburgh Press, 1961. Pp. 10—44.

Pryor, Hugh Clark. "Spelling." In *Minimum Essentials in Elementary School Subjects—Standards and Common Practices,* edited by S. Chester Parker, pp. 78—89. Bloomington, Illinois: Public School Publishing Co., 1919.

Read, Allen Walker. "The Spelling Bee: A Linguistic Institution of the American Folk." *PMLA* 56 (June 1941): 495—512.

Read, Charles. *Children's Categorization of Speech Sounds in English.* NCTE Research Report, no. 17. Urbana, Illinois: National Council of Teachers of English, 1975. [ED 112 426]

Rice, J. M. "The Futility of the Spelling Grind." *The Forum* 23 (March, August 1897): 409—19.

Rinsland, Henry D. *A Basic Vocabulary of Elementary School Children.* New York: MacMillan Co., 1945.

Santayana, George. *The Life of Reason; or, The Phases of Human Progress.* 5 vols. 2nd ed. New York: C. Scribner's Sons, 1928—1930.

Selke, Erich. "A Study of the Vocabulary of Ten Spellers." *The Elementary School Journal* 29 (June 1929): 767—70.

Sherwin, J. Stephen. *Four Problems in Teaching English: A Critique of Research.* Scranton, Pennsylvania: International Textbook Co., 1969. Pp. 29—108. [ED 029 867]

Shoemaker, Ervin C. *Noah Webster: Pioneer of Learning.* New York: Columbia University Press, 1936.

Simon, Dorothea P., and Simon, Herbert A. "Alternative Uses of Phonemic Information in Spelling." *Review of Educational Research* 43 (winter 1973): 115—37.

Smith, Nila Banton. *American Reading Instruction.* Newark, Delaware: International Reading Association, 1965.

Sudweeks, Joseph. "Practical Helps in Teaching Spelling: Summary of Helpful Principles and Methods." *Journal of Educational Research* 16 (September 1927): 106—18.

The New England Primer. Printed by E. Draper, ca. 1785. Twentieth Century Reprint. Boston: Ginn and Co., n.d.

Thorndike, Edward L., and Lorge, Irving. *The Teacher's Word Book of 30,000 Words.* New York: Teachers College, Columbia University, 1944.

Towery, Gene McGee. "A History of Spelling Instruction in America." Doctoral dissertation, Florida State University, 1971.

Venezky, Richard L. "English Orthography: Its Graphical Structure and Its Relation to Sound." *Reading Research Quarterly* 2 (1967): 75—106.

Composition:
Prospect and Retrospect

ALVINA TREUT BURROWS
Emeritus, New York University

Hodges's clear view of the history of spelling instruction, in the preceding chapter, demonstrates the emphasis on accuracy that has been the hallmark of such instruction since our earliest schools were established. Recent work in language development and psycholinguistics points toward possible modification of the goal of "perfect spelling" in all writing. Present-day focus on the skills needed to cope with and to enjoy our intricately communicating society shows the common sense of different requirements at different times. Obviously, there are many occasions that require legibility and spelling accuracy: for adults and adolescents—filling out employment application forms, writing business letters, keeping permanent records of many kinds; for children—furnishing their addresses and telephone numbers, ordering products through the mail, writing letters, and writing materials of many kinds for display on bulletin boards. But first drafts of stories, essays, and other creative ventures—even those of our country's founders—do not show the perfect or near-perfect conventions of later published form. To demand complete correctness from individuals first putting ideas on paper is unrealistic and counterproductive.

In this chapter, primary attention is paid to the main goal of communicating with one's audience through composition, using spelling as a component skill. Examples of young children's efforts to spell are shown in some detail in one study of composing processes (Graves 1973). The relationship of spelling to communicating is assumed as one concern, both in school and out. One spells to write purposefully, not just to get high scores on tests or to write lists of words from dictation. Correct form and legibility in letters, edited drafts, and other public writing seems a reasonable goal. However, other goals in teaching composition, in terms of both values and procedures, also are important. Thus a first question about current research in the writing of children and adolescents appears in briefest terms to be *where are we now?* A second query seeks certain milestones in composition and research: *how did we get here?* Another question is directed toward present needs for research: *what next?* And fourth and last is a question directed toward improving research in the study of the writing of children and adolescents: *how do we do it?* To illustrate this last subtopic, one investigation is reported in some detail as a model, and two others are sketched more briefly.

RECENT AND CURRENT RESEARCH DIRECTIONS

What is the concern of current research in the writing of children and adolescents? A preponderance of recent investigation undoubtedly is devoted to syntax. In view of the focus of linguistic scholarship in the last two decades, this cannot be surprising.

Emphasis grows also from an awareness that oral language precedes writing, both historically, in diverse cultures, and individually, in human development. Studies by Strickland (1962) and by Loban (1963) of children's oral syntax at various ages received rightful acclaim. Both revealed growth in productivity and in complexity. Loban, moreover, included samples of the writing of individuals in middle and secondary school. O'Donnell, Griffin, and Norris (1967) went a step further by comparing oral and written syntax in response to the same stimulus, in grades three, five, and seven. This study, however, employed a smaller sample and a smaller number of variables. Hunt (1964) published his study of syntax and his identification of the *minimal terminable unit* (T-unit) as "one main clause plus the subordinate clauses attached to or imbedded within it."

Writing sentences or T-units is undoubtedly an important component of written discourse. Greater sentence or T-unit length and an increased number of dependent clauses used by children as they mature gives a foundation for instructional emphases at successive age/grade levels. Evidence of individual differences within age groups adds further to our notions of the wide range of capabilities in writing, as in other areas of learning, in every grouping of youngsters brought together for instruction. Homogeneity becomes an ever more elusive concept.

Knowledge of some details of the acquisition and development of written syntax helps to enrich a picture of originality in sentence formation, as sketched by Naom Chomsky, whose removal of the development of oral expression from the realm of pure imitation has now become classic. Although, as a result of Chomsky's postulation, the utterance of original sentences by a young child has achieved the respect it merits, modification of Chomsky's stance is also accepted by some observers.

Findings of Strickland, of O'Donnell and others, of Loban, and of Hunt derived from the study of groups of learners. These revealed developmental tendencies to be shown by classes and age groups responding to given stimuli. But detailed accounts of the behavior of individuals as they write were lacking. True, vignettes and case studies had been included in prior works based upon actual productions, anecdotes, and descriptions of the student as a person. Moreover, some had included individual accounts against a backdrop of classroom and community. But, for the most part, such anecdotal and sample reports could not stand up to the criteria of rigorous research. In-depth studies of individuals at work remained for current scholars, and some outstanding work of this kind will be reported as examples for replication and extension.

Evaluation has been, and continues to be, an involved and difficult matter to examine objectively. Problems of evaluator consistency remain serious, although techniques have been devised for determining the degree to which such consistency can be acquired (Braddock and others 1963). A new and more detailed procedure for rating the compositions of children was presented by Tway (1970) in her doctoral study, in which she developed a literary rating scale and validated its use by teachers. However, this is relevant to imaginative narrative, not to the full range of children's writing. Other evaluation procedures and studies are currently in progress.

Concern for motivation is beginning to generate some studies aimed at what induces young people to write and how differing motivations seem to affect resulting compositions. Some of these investigations combine an immediate stimulus with motivation that is inherently distinct from requirement, assignment, and other kinds of stimulus, although, of course, it has some bearing on the basic human urge to communicate.

In sum, then, current research appears to be making some strides in examining the processes and components of writing, in defining its many related variables, in discerning various developmental phenomena, and in arriving at more nearly definitive evaluation of methods of teaching. Contrast with the major concerns of the 1920s is dramatic. During that period of prolific research, the goals were the examination of length of sentences, number of complete versus incomplete sentences, total number of words, and number of different words, or "type/token" ratio.

HISTORICAL BACKGROUND—WITH GAPS

How did we get from *then* to *now*, or, in somewhat more professional terms, what are some of the important milestones in composition research? It seems wise to look first at the compendia that summarize research studies and serve as tools for investigators surveying the growing amount of research literature. Possibly the first catalog of research in elementary children's composition was the bulletin *Children's Writing: Research in Composition and Related Skills*, prepared by the National Conference on Research in English (NCRE). Outdated as that summary now is, it is useful in showing the thinking of the research leaders of the 1950s, many of whom, still researching, have moved far beyond what they then perceived. A committee of seven contributors was chaired by Burrows (1960—1961). Each of the six main contributors presented briefs of the major investigations in his or her field—composition in primary grades, composition in intermediate grades, grammar in language teaching, handwriting in children's composition, or research in spelling. Aimed at bringing together reports of outstanding studies in the twentieth century and unifying some of the disparate findings, this catalog and interpretation are now a historic milestone.

In 1961, the American Educational Research Association published *Review of Educational Research, Language and Fine Arts*. Summaries of research in curriculum, in the teaching of composition, in evaluation, in grammar and usage, in spelling, in handwriting, and in linguistics were prepared by DeBoer (1961), who had done the section on grammar and usage in the NCRE bulletin of 1960—1961. Each of the seven areas was treated more briefly than in the previous review, but one new area, then growing in importance, was added: linguistics.

Seeking to make the findings of research more readable and more readily applicable by classroom teachers, the American Educational Research Association and the National Education Association combined efforts to do a series on research in teaching in many curriculum areas. A selective summary and interpretation, *Teaching Composition*, was first published in 1959 and was revised in 1963 (Burrows). Whether this and its companion bulletins succeeded at all in narrowing the gap between research and practice is not known, although some of the bulletins were translated into other languages and were published in revised editions.

Far more extensive and thorough was *Research in Written Composition*, published by the National Council of Teachers of English. The final report was written by Braddock, Lloyd-Jones, and Schoer (1963), all of the University of Iowa. A committee of eight assembled to plan the scope of the work and to select the means of surveying the array of research studies conducted in this country and abroad. Several grants supported the production, which covered research in elementary and secondary school composition. In addition to a search for worthy investigations at the universities represented by the committee, a screening was done of materials known to a much wider circle of teachers and scholars. Criteria of excellence in research were defined, and, of the 485 studies selected for careful scrutiny, 5 were chosen as fulfilling most of those criteria. Even in this small number, exemplifying rigorous standards, some "slips" were allowed, and such allowances were carefully noted. Again in print, this significant document is a "must" for serious students of composition research.

The most recent summary of written composition was made by an NCRE committee headed by Sara Lundsteen (1976). This summary, *Help for the Teacher of Written Composition*, published by NCRE and the ERIC Clearinghouse on Reading and Communications Skills, includes recent investigations in composition, in both elementary and secondary schools.

As the title of the present volume suggests, it seems in order to attempt a sketch of a few of the milestones in actual teaching, whether or not related to research, which just possibly have been the irritants that spurred some curious souls to find out how and why composing is done.

The bicentennial year suggested a beginning point for historical views —but only *suggested.* Blame for including only the second of the two centuries must be laid at my feet. What happened from 1776 to 1876 is a darkness yet to be illuminated by even a single candle. Truly, very little is available at the moment to show actual writing by children and adolescents for even the nineteenth century, and, at the moment, only one example is in my possession:

January 1, 1872

My dear Parents,

On this happy morning I come before you to present my sincere wishes Happy, happy New Year to you! I feel how your loving kindness has guarded every day of my life, and how little I do to prove my love and gratitude. But you are so kind, you overlook all my faults, and when I promise to do better, you forgive me at once. As I know that nothing would make you so happy as to see me an obedient, dutiful daughter, I will try my utmost to please you and my teachers by applying myself to every task that is given me so that I may be a pleasure and a comfort to you. May God bless you; may he give you health, happiness, and may you enjoy many happy days together is the wish of your loving daughter.

Sophie

A description of the procedures by which this demonstration of filial piety was achieved was furnished by no less a figure than H. L. Mencken (who attended the same school as did Sophie) in his book *Happy Days* (1940). The writer of the letter, then a little girl of ten years, later pronounced Mencken's description "exactly the way we did it." Sophie in 1872 and Mencken in 1886 were treated to the same kind of "composing" lesson—obviously, the copying of their teacher's composition. The writer of the quoted letter could later remember no instance of independent writing of any kind. When and where the opportunity to set individual ideas down on paper was first granted remains to be discovered. In the diaries and biographies of some authors, in both England and the U.S., children's writing of individuality and charm is to be found. It is difficult to say how the schools treated problems of composing, if they did at all.

Bronson Alcott, father of Louisa May Alcott and now more famous than ever, wrote in his journals some of his views about the teaching of writing. He observed that if young children's handwriting is small and cramped, the children must have been made fearful, and this restriction is not "natural." Since his four daughters were tutored at home, by himself and by Thoreau and Emerson, their excellence in composing cannot be attributed to the very few years they spent in formal schooling.

Both before and after the Civil War, great gaps are evident. What continuity, if any, existed between the practices of outstanding teachers, from colonial times until the post—Civil War period? This is an area yet to be examined and described using the letters and diaries of adults and young people of the period, the recollections of living adults, and the journals of teachers and educational leaders. Courses of study during that period are another primary source, although what was prescribed by officials and what was actually done in classes could be very different. Were teachers and parents concerned with originality or only with correct form? Were some teachers concentrating exclusively on preparation of the elite for college here or abroad?

TEXT BOOKS AND TEACHERS' REFERENCES

The evolution of textbooks constitutes yet another source through which to trace concern for the changing needs of young children and adolescents. It does not seem possible at the present time to construct an adequate picture of the appearance of texts for teaching composition, to say nothing of relating those texts to philosophies dominant at various periods of social and educational history. Though the importance of reading instruction was richly represented in early hornbooks and primers, as far back as the colonial period of American history, the paucity, or perhaps even the absence, of composition texts for school children throughout the 1800s needs to be thoroughly researched.

The view that writing was as natural as talking seemed to be assumed by Davis (1839) in one of the early books on methods. This slender volume began with a discussion of the duties of parents and teachers and followed with chapters on school government and on individual differences. It then proceeded with separate chapters on teaching the alphabet, spelling, defining words, grammar, arithmetic, geography, and the use of illustration and apparatus and concluded with a chapter on moral education and the Bible. But it gave no space to instruction in composition. Teachers were advised to have copies and pens ready for penmanship; the practical and humane admonition was given to schedule such instruction (during the winter) for the latter part of the morning, when the ink would no longer be frozen, and not in the late afternoon, when children's hands would tremble from the cold. Davis went on to say:

> How pleasant to be able to communicate our thoughts to absent friends! how useful to be able to record the results of business! how wonderful to be able to put our thoughts on paper, that they may be communicated to minds in other lands and in other ages!

But he gave no advice as to how this art was to be taught. Indeed, one must assume, from present minimal evidence, that composition as we now perceive it simply was not taught. Handwriting and spelling, yes; but how to help children set down their ideas and feelings on paper for a live and known audience was ignored in professional references and very probably in the classroom. Not until the early years of the twentieth century did the schools begin this task.

That early twentieth century texts in language included instruction in composing is evident from historical collections. When did the apparently great emphasis put by early publications upon correct punctuation and spelling, along with proper margins and clear penmanship, give way to a balanced emphasis upon content or even on sentence formation? To what extent did texts set the pace for changing practice? To what extent did pioneer schools forge ahead of more conventional ones? How did the developing field of textbooks relate to such basic position statements as the famed Hosic (1917) report and the experience curriculum (Hatfield 1935), just two milestone documents by acknowledged leaders?

FAMOUS COMMISSIONS ON THE TEACHING OF ENGLISH

In an article surveying the history of creative expression, Kantor (1975) began with the late nineteenth-century publication of the justly famous *Report of the Committee of Ten*, of which the prestigious president of Harvard University, Charles W. Eliot (1894), was the chair. Scarcely a better choice of historic documents could be made, either for Kantor's purposes or for the substance of this review. The report of the Committee of Ten is quite possibly the first written summation of a committee's point of view about the teaching of English throughout the elementary grades and high school. Although its main focus was upon secondary education, the committee reasoned that elementary school must prepare pupils for the high school curriculum. The following excerpts from the report of the subcommittee on English, known as the Conference on the Teaching of English, presented the view of that body on the goals and the methods of teaching composition in the entire elementary school.

To THE COMMITTEE OF TEN:—

The Conference on the Study of English has the honor to submit the following Report:—

The Conference was called to order on Wednesday, December 28th, 1892, at quarter of eleven A.M., by Professor Allen. Principal Thurber was elected Chairman and Professor Kittredge, Secretary. The Conference remained in session till half past three o'clock Friday, December 30th, when it adjourned *sine die*. Every member was present at the deliberations and took part in debate. The results embodied in the present Report were arrived at after much discussion, and represent in all but a few points of minor importance the unanimous opinion of the Conference. The subjects which the Conference thought were included in its commission are those usually taught in schools under the names of English Language, English Grammar, Composition, Rhetoric, and English Literature. Elocution appeared to lie outside of the subjects which the meeting was convened to discuss.

The main direct objects of the teaching of English in schools seems to be two: (1) to enable the pupil to understand the expressed thoughts of others and to give expression to thoughts of his own; and (2) to cultivate a taste for reading, to give the pupil some acquaintance with good literature, and to furnish him with the means of extending that acquaintance. Incidentally, no doubt, a variety of other ends may be subserved by English study, but such subsidiary interests should never be allowed to encroach on the two main purposes just indicated. Further, though it may be necessary to consider these main purposes separately in the Report or even to separate them formally in the statement of a programme, yet in practice they should never be dissociated in the mind of the teacher and their mutual dependence should be kept constantly present to the mind of the pupils. The recommendations of the Conference should all be interpreted in accordance with these general principles, which were never lost sight of in its debates.

The recommendations of the Conference fall naturally into two divisions: (1) English in schools below the high-school grade, and (2) English in the high-school.

I. THE STUDY OF ENGLISH IN SCHOOLS BELOW THE HIGH-SCHOOL GRADE

If the pupil is to secure control of the language as an instrument for the expression of his thoughts, it is necessary (1) that, during the period of life when imitation is the chief motive principle in education, he should be kept so far as possible away from the influence of bad models and under the influence of good models, and (2) that every thought which he expresses, whether orally or on paper, should be regarded as a proper subject for criticism as to language. Thus every lesson in geography or physics or mathematics may and should become a part of the pupil's training in English. There can be no more appropriate moment for a brief lesson in expression than the moment when the pupil has something which he is trying to express. If this principle is not regarded, a recitation in history or in botany, for example, may easily undo all that a set exercise in English has accomplished. In order that both teacher and pupil may attach due importance to this incidental instruction in English, the pupil's standing in any subject should depend in part on his use of clear and correct English.

In addition to this incidental training, appropriate special instruction in English should form a part of the curriculum from the beginning. For convenience this special instruction may be considered under three heads: (a) "language" and composition, (b) formal or systematic grammar, (c) reading, or lessons in literature.

A. "Language" and composition.—During the *first two years* at school, children may acquire some fluency of expression by reproducing orally in their own words stories told them by their teachers and by inventing stories about objects and pictures.

Not later than the first term of the *third school-year* children should begin to compose in writing. To assist them in overcoming mechanical difficulties (as of punctuation, the use of capitals, etc.), they should be required to copy and to write from dictation and from memory short and easy passages of prose and verse.

From the beginning of the *third* to the end of the *sixth* school-year, "language-work" should be of three kinds:

1. Oral and written exercises in the correct employment of the forms of the so-called "irregular" verbs, of pronominal forms, and of words and phrases frequently misused.

2. Oral and written exercises in the most elementary form of composition, that is, in the construction of sentences of various kinds. The matter out of which the sentences are to be constructed may, if necessary, be supplied by the teacher; but the pupil should, from his earliest years, be encouraged to furnish his own material, expressing his own thoughts in a natural way. The greatest care should be taken to make these exercises practical rather than technical and to avoid the errors of the old-fashioned routine method of instruction in grammar.

3. The writing of narratives and descriptions.—These exercises should begin with the *third school-year* and should be continued throughout the course. The subjects assigned should gradually increase in difficulty: in the *seventh and eighth school-years*, if not earlier, they may often be suggested by the pupil's observation or personal experience. The paraphrasing of poetry is not to be commended as an exercise in prose composition: it is often of value to require the pupil to tell or write, in his own words, the story of some narrative poem; but the reducing of lyric poetry to prose is hardly to be defended. Pains should be taken, from the outset, to enlarge and improve the child's vocabulary by suggesting to him, for the expression of his thoughts, better words than those he may himself have chosen. He should be trained to recognize when a sentence naturally closes, and should be warned against running distinct sentences together. He should also be trained to perceive the larger divisions of thought which are conventionally indicated by paragraphs. The teacher should bear in mind that the necessity of correctness in the formation of sentences and paragraphs is like the necessity of accurate addition, subtraction, multiplication, and division in mathematical work, and that composition proper,—the grouping of sentences and paragraphs,—as well as development of a central idea, should never be taught until this basis of correct sentences is attained.

Spelling should be learned incidentally, in connection with every subject studied, and not from a spelling-book.

Compositions and all other written exercises should receive careful and appropriate criticism, and the staff of instructors should be large enough to protect every teacher from an excess of this peculiarly exacting and fatiguing work. (Pp. 86—88)

———————————

For elementary and secondary school, the report recommended that content and method preserve tradition and adopt a few changes. To the doctrine of mental discipline was added the ideal of social efficiency. Though this seems a small and reluctant step forward to viewers from the last quarter of the twentieth century, it must be remembered that the document was written just thirty years after the Civil War and during the last triumphant decade of the reign of Queen Victoria. As late as the 1920s, the *Committee of Ten Report* was revered in some circles, and its precepts shaped curriculum work in a number of schools.

A few professional references in the late 1890s and in the first decade of this century recommended the inclusion of spontaneity and freedom in the teaching of writing. The notion of writing for a particular audience appeared at about this time, as did the writing of poetry.

The next milestone in a sequence of national reports by concerned specialists was the Hosic report, so-called for its chairman, James F. Hosic (1917). *Report on the Reorganization of English in the Secondary Schools* made a considerable departure from the academic requirements of the Committee of Ten document. Referring to the highly formal requirements of college entrance examinations and their lack of relation to students' lives, Hosic and his committee took a clear stand against formal discipline as the sole principle activating the selection of high school English content:

> Like the preceding commissions, the committee on college entrance requirements made a report which tended to foster a type of English study that practically ignored oral composition and subjects of expression drawn from the pupil's own experience, and that constantly applied in the study of literary masterpieces formal rhetorical categories. A reaction against such a type of study was inevitable.
>
> With the wonderful development of the public high school during the last two decades that reaction has come. From its beginning the high school was fighting ground. Established, like the academy, to provide a greater variety of studies than the preparatory school, it was soon itself called upon to furnish the opportunity for college preparation. Funds were hardly adequate to carry on courses both for those who were going to college and those who were not, and in the end the definite desires of the college-preparatory group triumphed. The effect was to render the English work excessively formal in character.
>
> This was due in large part to the dogma of formal discipline, which the colleges insisted upon as the essential element in preparation long after they had partly discarded it for themselves. Studies must be hard and disagreeable and a certain amount of ground must be covered in order that the mind of youth should be steeled for the intellectual encounters to be met with in college days. This was the ideal which had justified

emphasis upon the classics and mathematics, and it was insisted upon also for English; and this without regard to the fact that the term English covered such diverse subjects as grammar, composition, literature, history of literature, history of language, spelling, etymology, etc. (P. 15)

The report of the Committee on Composition of the Hosic Commission detailed the kinds of learning experiences in composition deemed suitable for pupils in grades ten through twelve.

REPORT OF THE COMMITTEE ON COMPOSITION IN THE TENTH, ELEVENTH, AND TWELFTH GRADES (SENIOR HIGH SCHOOL).

I. PURPOSES OF TEACHING COMPOSITION.

The purpose of teaching composition is to enable the pupil to speak and write correctly, convincingly, and interestingly. The first step toward efficiency in the use of language is the cultivation of earnestness and sincerity; the second is the development of accuracy and correctness; the third is the arousing of individuality and artistic consciousness.

A definite point of view must be kept in mind by the teacher if this general aim is to be realized; that point of view is that he must meet the needs of the individual pupil. The development of the expressional powers of the individual pupil should be the aim of the teacher rather than the teaching of specific form and rules. Each year of a pupil's life brings a broader outlook through added experience and more mature thought. Each year, consequently, there is need for an increased mastery of technique and of more mature forms of expression. Only from a realization on the part of the teacher of this growth of personality can an adequate course in composition be organized.

Such individual treatment requires that each pupil do much writing and speaking on subjects familiar to him. If material for oral and written work is taken from the experience of the pupil, familiarity with the subject will enable him (a) to give attention to correctness rather than to the mastery of the thought, (b) to speak or write convincingly by reason of his own interest, (c) to give some attention to the arrangement and presentation of his thoughts in a manner likely to arouse interest in others.

The classroom activities in teaching composition when arranged in the order of their importance are: (a) Letter writing; (b) relating of some simple incidents and explanation of familiar subjects; (c) analysis of pieces of writing; (d) reports; (e) literary composition; (f) debate.

Letter writing is placed first as being of most importance, since it is the form of writing the pupil will use most frequently. The pupil should be able to write a courteous letter according to the forms in general use, and of the degree of formality or informality appropriate to the occasion. Second in order of importance is exposition. The second aim, then, is to train the pupil to compose a clear and readable paragraph or series of paragraphs on familiar subject matter, with due observance of unity and order and with some specific details. Third, is the ability to analyze and present in outline form the gist of a lecture or piece of literature, and to expand such an outline. The fourth aim comes when the pupil is more mature and has developed in power of expression. He should be able, with due time for study and preparation, to plan and work out a clear, well-ordered, and interesting report of some length upon his special interests—literary, scientific, commercial, or what not. These four aims should be kept in mind for all pupils. Other aims should be kept in mind for those who have special aptitudes; for those who have the argumentative mind, ability to arrange the material for a debate in an effective way; for those who have literary tastes, ability to write a short story or other bit of imaginative composition, with some vigor and personality of style and in proper form to be submitted for publication, and to arrange suitable stories in form for dramatic presentation.

The above aims have to do chiefly with content and the arrangement of the thought for effectiveness. It must be remembered also that correctness as to formal details is an aim throughout. These details are: A legible and firm handwriting, correct spelling, correctness in grammar and idiom, and observance of the ordinary rules for capitals and marks of punctuation. These, however, being not specifically literary, but the essentials of good workmanship in all kinds of written work, are the concern of all teachers, and should be enforced in all classes by the authority of the principal. Beyond these general requirements the writer should, through his English work, make an effort to gain an enlarged vocabulary through reading and to use a vocabulary in his written work suitable to his audience and the occasion. A concise and vigorous style may often be gained unconsciously by the reading of authors who possess these qualities, but mere imitation of style may result in "fine writing." A pupil may be set for work on the same project, however, that an author has worked out if there is no conscious effort to use phrases or words that are not his own. Firmness and flexibility in writing may be gained by reconstructing sentences and paragraphs of one's composition.

II. CLASSROOM ACTIVITIES.

Classroom activities in composition should be founded upon and should grow out of the experience of the pupils. These experiences may be classified as follows:

1. Those that school life provides:
   (a) School work.
   (b) School activities, social and athletic.
2. Those that outside interests provide:
   (a) Work—past, present, and future.
   (b) Amusements, play.

    (c) Interests in the home.

    (d) Other interests, as travel and local industries.

    (e) Reading.

School work itself furnishes a vast amount of material for composition. Heretofore there has been a tendency to base much of the theme work on the English classics. The introduction of the sciences and of vocational training, however, has made a great amount of material growing out of the actual experience of the pupils available. There is a growing tendency to use this material and to reduce greatly the amount of composition work based on the classics.

All theme work should be made as real and vital as possible. The following examples illustrate how school work may be adapted to this purpose and suggest methods of giving practice in different types of discourse. A pupil makes a field trip with his geography class; this trip furnishes more vital narrative material than "A visit to England at the time of Ivanhoe;" it is fresher material even than "Last year's fishing trip." Another visits a big chemical factory; extreme interest in the subject will tend to produce a good description of the factory. A third becomes interested in radium in the physics class. He reads all that he can find and assembles his knowledge in a good exposition. A senior has devoted some time to deciding what he will do after he leaves the high school. An argument in defense of his decision, whether for a certain college or for a certain vocation, has as its basis the mental experience of the pupil himself.

Outside interests—play, amusements, work, home activities, reading —will furnish a vast amount of material if the teacher is able to direct the pupils to it. For example, in the class is a boy living in a crowded section of the city who has taken a prize for having the best home garden. He tells how to have a successful garden. A boy whose father is assistant to the city forester has a collection of moths and writes well about these beautiful creatures. The list of such topics is well-nigh unlimited, and they are extremely interesting to the class. Moreover, the pupils feel that these topics are worthy of their efforts. Such exercises can often be presented before the entire school, sometimes with stereopticon views.

The sports furnish good subjects; for instance, a talk on "Swimming" might be given by the boy who takes the prizes in the contests; or on "How to win a foot race," by the boy who won a race in a field-day contest. In general, subjects should be suggested, not assigned.

For the very small minority who seem to have no developed interest, subjects may have to be assigned. Even in these cases a nucleus of interest may be found. A visitor in the house talks about the "glass industry." A boy listens and wants to know all about the subject. He reads (magazine articles preferred) and gives a talk, making the subject as interesting as possible, not a résumé of one article but assembled knowledge from many articles. Problems and questions of the hour may have interest for some who read the newspapers. This nucleus of interest should be in the mind of the pupil, not in the mind of the teacher. The problem of the teacher is to get at this nucleus.

Not only should the activities on which composition is based be real, not only should they touch the life of the pupil in some way through interest or experience, but the exercises themselves should have, as far as possible, a purpose. Much of the work in English may be used for definite ends in the school itself. A school paper and an annual furnish means of presenting the best poems, stories, and editorials produced in the English classes. By skillful management the local newspapers may be induced to publish some of these exercises. In large cities a report of school athletics is made for the local papers every week by pupils, who often receive remuneration. Programs may be arranged for the presentation before the school of the class work in English. Speeches of acceptance at the awarding of medals for various sports may be given as class exercises; and so may the after-dinner speeches for class banquets.

The orientation of the English work should be the constant aim of the teacher. The pupil will be able to get freedom of expression if he chooses an audience, and does not write with the vision of a teacher, blue pencil in hand, looking over his shoulder.

The activities so far described have a value in that they are likely to produce clear and definite expression. They also furnish material for organization. What the organization of the material shall be is determined in each case by the purpose in view and the audience for whom the composition is prepared. Now, by carefully outlining each subject the pupil learns unity without being burdened with rules. By working out details with the help of the outline he learns coherence and emphasis in the same way.

To sum up: In the composition course, content should appeal to the pupil as first in importance; organization, second; details of punctuation, spelling, sentence structure, choice of words (matters of careful scrutiny), third.

Besides these general and practical activities, there are certain others by means of which special capabilities may be developed. Fact writing and imaginative writing come from two types of mind. The pupil who can write a short story should be given an opportunity and should have special training, but excellence in short-story writing, or even fair work, should not be made a standard for passing pupils, nor should inability to write a fair story be made a basis for failure. All pupils should be encouraged to try, however, otherwise ability in this line may not be discovered. Many times this ability can be discovered early in the course. If a pupil can tell an incident or write a good description showing "vigor and personality," he is likely to be the one who can manage a short story. Some trials at verse writing will reveal pupils who have ability in this direction. The same is true of dramatization. Easy exercises in the writing of conversation that shows character will reveal pupils who, with special training, can dramatize. Here again the work, i.e., dramatization, should be based on the interests of the pupils. Material for dramatization may often be found in local history.

In short, there should be frequent exercises in imaginative writing as "trials" in the early years of the high school. Special training in dramatization, advertisement writing, journalism, and short-story writing should be placed in the last year.

What has been said of the short story is also true of debating—not every pupil has the debating mind. The one who has will discover himself in classroom argument and should be encouraged by the teacher to debate. Debating societies, where the pupils take the initiative, should be organized for those who can profit by them.

Pictures may be used at any time to suggest a theme or a train of thought. Some profitable work may be done by the use of the right type of picture. For example, the cartoon may often be used for the development of a short theme. The chief editorial of the day in many newspapers is often put into the cartoon.

Letter writing should be a frequent class exercise. Pupils should be given constant practice in the writing of letters that have a real purpose; the body of the letter should grow out of the interest of the pupils. The boys take more interest in ordering a bill of goods from "Spalding's" than books from a publishing company. The boy who has a garden would prefer to write for seeds. Letters of application should, if possible, be written for real positions, to real persons. Invitations to school parties and banquets should be made class exercises. Letters may, in some cases, be written to the principal asking for class standings.

The spirit of informal letter writing may be stimulated by the simpler letters of Stevenson, Dickens, Carroll, and Lincoln. The pupil should feel that in the letter he has absolute freedom to write on a familiar subject, with more revelation of personal feelings and tastes than in any other form. The problem is to show the pupil that he has mental and emotional experiences worth while putting into a letter.

The chief forms should be as familiar as the multiplication table. A letter that has one inadmissible feature in heading, salutation, or closing deserves censure.

Oral composition is growing in favor. Ability to think on one's feet and to express one's thoughts clearly, forcibly, and persuasively, should be the aim. Like the written work, this oral work should be definite and have a purpose. A class of boys, for example, sees a definite value in being trained to explain "how to make a weld" as a foreman must explain it to apprentices. It is not difficult for them to see that the one who interests his audience (the class), who holds their attention by his clear, distinct articulation and orderly presentation will very likely be able to control the men put in his charge. Young people are severe critics. Their vote of "good" or "bad" is a great incentive. Many excellent pupils who have for two years of their school life recited from five to ten minutes in a connected, orderly manner are often able to say but a few words, and those in a confused

manner, when called upon to face a class. Oral composition is almost val-
ueless unless the pupil stands before the class. Thirty pairs of strange,
questioning, doubting, curious eyes are more terrifying than one familiar,
critical pair that the pupil has been in the habit of reciting to, and hence
the pupil gains valuable self-control in learning to face them. An exercise
where presence, showing dignity and control, is essential, makes a direct
appeal to pupils. In such exercises the pupil finds himself and gains initiative. The oral work should be continuous throughout the course, not
made up of just a few lessons for a few weeks. The aim should be development of power to think before an audience and to find the language in
which to express oneself.

In general, the classroom activities in composition should spring from
the life of the pupil and should develop in him the power to express his
individual experiences. In order to assist in meeting these requirements a
course has been suggested which includes for each year (a) specific aims;
(b) a collection of suitable material; (c) suggestions as to method applicable to the material. (Pp. 54—59)

The Hosic report may well be the first national committee report
to cite in a quasi-official document some relationship between speaking
and writing. For the early high school years, the committee recommended
imaginative exercises as "trials," to select students of talent for further
training in literary writing in grade twelve. Such training was to consist of
the writing of short stories, drama, and verse.

To understand some of the pronouncements of this report, one must
envision a nation engaged in the First World War, a world in which mon-
archy was waning but still was being fought for. Education of the elite
and selectivity in education dominated even public-school thinking. College
was for the wealthy and for a few lucky, hard-working, and gifted young
men and for even fewer women.

It is indicative of the upheaval of the time that just seventeen years
after the Hosic report came a document representing views of teachers
who chaired active committees of the National Council of Teachers of
English (NCTE). Entitled *An Experience Curriculum* (Hatfield 1935), this
important document illustrated a sweeping forward movement. Even its
name dramatized its departure from the strictures of formal discipline.
Whereas the Committee of Ten in 1894 had not emphasized writing about
personal experiences until grades seven and eight ("if not earlier"), the
Hatfield report suggested such writing begin in grade one, closely allied
with oral composing, drama, and exposure to literature. Obviously, creativity was given a much larger role. Not restricted to pupils of talent, originality was to be supported by specifically described experiences in observing,
imagining, and reflecting. The commission under Hatfield's leadership also
distinguished between creative writing carried out for its intrinsic satisfactions and composition of a utilitarian nature, serving social communication
purposes.

The influence of *An Experience Curriculum* was of historic importance, although positions opposed to its emphasis on creativity and "real"
communication made themselves felt. Still another conflict arose between
forces advocating a return to a traditional Latin-based grammar and
proponents of the emerging science of linguistics. The old contest continued
between training in the mechanics of writing and allowing a spontaneous,
personal writing. Some of the gulf continues to separate the proponents of
imaginative expression from the defenders of factual and business communication. However, the wealth of teaching ideas and the comprehensiveness
of the program delineated in 1935 by Hatfield and the NCTE Curriculum
Commission are still germane to curriculum development, promoting the
integration of writing with the entire language arts program and, indeed,
with the entire curriculum.

Other documents developed by leading teachers in the broad discipline of English at both elementary and secondary levels appeared as
organizations other than NCTE assumed responsibilities. In fact, concern
for composition in the curriculum extended to the college years, both
undergraduate and graduate divisions. An entire series of books on the
English curriculum was originated by NCTE, and in each the needs of
students and teachers were considered. This broad venture occupied many
years during the late 1950s and 1960s.

Concurrent with the completion of the last in the NCTE curriculum
volumes was a meeting of representatives from four organizations: NCTE,
the Modern Language Association, the American Studies Association, and
the College English Association. All levels of education were represented
by professors of English and of education, leaders of professional organizations, administrators, and a representative of the United States Department
of Health, Education, and Welfare. These leaders addressed the problems
of teaching English in the period following the Second World War, when
colleges and graduate schools were pressured by peak enrollments and
when it seemed necessary to reduce the time needed for doctoral-level
preparation, while maintaining high standards of knowledge, both in depth
and in breadth. Difficulties between pedagogy and content were debated,
as were the gains and dilemmas of cross-disciplinary studies.

The section of their report that dealt with writing at all levels was
the work of the several members of the Basic Issues Conference. This task
force was concerned with both the general and the specific problems of
composition teaching. The first meeting of the conference, in 1958, discussed current practices and problems at every level and age of schooling.
Smaller work sessions followed, and a final all-member meeting arrived at
agreement in principle for the published report of the conference on the
Basic Issues in the Teaching of English (1959). The problems included
were those of continuity, of differentiation of programs to meet student
needs during an age of ever-broadening social and economic student
populations, and of respect for standards of excellence. The teaching of
writing in elementary and secondary schools was considered to include
both imaginative and objective communication aspects. The *basic issues*

are still with us in 1977, both in theory and in practice. Indeed, some have become more acute.

SUPPORT FOR STUDIES OF COMPOSITION

Two other important activities carried on in the 1960s, when federal money for such projects was available, should be noted. One was Project English, a series of explorations in curriculum development, conducted largely at the University of Nebraska and at Northwestern University. The Nebraska Center related children's writing primarily to literature: children were to emulate literary models by extension, by paralleling, or by other means. Large, compendious reports were published as part of a government-sponsored project. A second and complementary activity also gained federal support during that decade. Workshops for teachers were carried on at many universities; some of them were aimed at helping teachers with their own writing. One series of workshops, which published useful data about its results, was held at the University of Georgia. Other workshops focused primarily on planning ways and means of including more opportunities for many kinds of writing. It must be recalled that this burgeoning of concern for composing took place at a time when elementary teachers were approaching "the new math" and much more work in science.

A counter effort, yet in some ways a complementary one, was the meeting of leaders from the United Kingdom and the United States at the Dartmouth Conference in 1966. Twenty-eight teachers from the United States, twenty from the United Kingdom, and one from Canada met in late August and early September under the auspices of NCTE, the Modern Language Association, and the British National Association for the Teaching of English. First-hand, informal accounts by some of the participants revealed the colorful, spirited, and, at times, acrimonious debates that took place that summer in Hanover, New Hampshire. The published report, *Growth through English* (Dixon 1967), revealed some of the consensus achieved and, to Dixon's credit, expressed regrets for the omission of some of the minority views. For both elementary and secondary years, a freer atmosphere for writing was espoused. The preservation of creativity was supported through acknowledgment of the need for more information about the apparent polarization of reality and fantasy in early adolescence.

A second report, *The Uses of English* (Muller 1967), presented a somewhat more structured array of principles and ways of putting them to work, ranging from fundamentals in chapter one, "What Is English?" through democracy in the classroom, mass media, and myths, to chapter ten, "The Issues of Responsibility." The influence of these two volumes is difficult to assess, but whatever the final opinion may be—if there be anything final in the realm of teaching—these reports will continue to present a portrait of the complexities of English teaching and learning.

If serious professional attention to research seems to have been rare—a conclusion that is well-nigh inescapable—there are now some encouraging signals. NCTE gives recognition at its annual convention to promising young researchers. The first such award was made in 1970, and, thus far, seven of these awards have been made for research in composition.

NCTE also originated a research foundation in 1960 and thus far has helped to support six projects dealing with composition research. The first subsidy was given in 1963, and the six studies now completed embrace a variety of problems. Yet another award made by NCTE began another venture of great service to researchers. The magazine *Elementary English*, devoted to the teaching of the language arts in elementary schools and published since 1975 under the title *Language Arts*, began a series of research summaries which included studies in composition. Various leaders in elementary education have authored these summary surveys. Appearing almost every year since 1957, they have become a valuable tool for investigators.

LEADERS AND CONTROVERSIES

Any historical overview of an educational movement, no matter how abbreviated, must include the work of leaders. Had there not been proponents and demonstrators of change, the work of commissions and councils and associations could not occur. In recalling great individual liberators of the writing of children and adolescents, the name Hughes Mearns immediately flashes before the mind. His books, *Creative Youth* (1929) and *Creative Power* (1958, 1975) have become beacons to those fumbling toward the freeing of young people's originality, to those who know by intuition and observation that there must be more to teaching than marking corrections on students' papers. Gifted teacher and humane counselor, Mearns was also a novelist and a charming, gracious speaker with a gentle and contagious sense of humor. Another great contributor to the concern for teaching composition along with the whole complex of literacy was Dora V. Smith. Her doctoral study (1928) of high school children's composition was followed by a vigorous career in writing, in teaching, and in nationwide lecturing and consulting. Perhaps the climax of this challenging life was a world tour in search of manuscripts written by natives of the developing nations after World War II. The names Harold Rugg, John T. Frederick, James Hosic, Luella Cook, Louis La Brant, and others as far back as Hinsdale (1898) deserve many pages. And nearly all leaders from the turn of the century until today would want, no doubt, to pay tribute to John Dewey. His contribution to philosophy and to education continues to extend far beyond the borders of America and beyond the limits of his long life. His influence was, and is, a galvanic power in the progress toward freedom and discipline in education.

It would be a distortion of fact, however, to weave a magic carpet of great names and to fly on it through the history of composition teaching in this century, without acknowledging crosscurrents and strong headwinds. Continuity and evolution emerge as in any historical study, but regression occurs as well as progress. Indeed, it appears that action has regularly been followed by reaction, as cited in the well-known physical law, though in historical perspective reaction is not always opposite and equal. Here again, names flash to mind: The titles *Quackery in the Public Schools* (Lynd 1950) and *Educational Wastelands* (Bestor 1953) became something of a slogan, if not quite a battlecry, for those groups wanting a return to "the good old days." Though serving as a rallying point for many who opposed change on principle, these books brought many communities to the vigorous examination of their schools for the first time since the rapid expansion following World War II. Debates in parent-teacher groups "waxed wroth." "My child can't spell" and "My child is in high school and still can't write a decent sentence" were complaints frequently heard. Many shades of community leadership gave expression to a plethora of diverse opinion among teachers.

Fortunately, money was still available in the sixties and early seventies for considerable experimentation. It is hoped that the period of economic stringency of the mid-seventies will prove a clearing period for beliefs and methods. Perhaps a few years of less violent controversy may effect a meeting of minds and produce greater satisfactions for teachers and pupils. A clearer realization of goals of English teaching in general and of composition in particular might lead to clearer research directions.

PRESENT STATUS IN COMPOSITION RESEARCH

No formal survey is available, but it is safe to say that more research in composition is now going on in universities in the U.S. than ever before, even more than during the productive decades of the 1920s and 1960s. This is true in part because relatively little was done earlier. Research in reading started long before research in composition gained much ground. Other fields of English also received greater attention. One cannot say that composition research has achieved parity with these fields, but certainly progress has been and is being made. The study of linguistics has contributed considerable impetus to this robust growth. Many studies have been done in children's written syntax and in developmental sequences in that syntax. Hunt's identification of the "T-unit" (1963) and O'Donnell, Griffin, and Norris's (1967) comparison of the oral and written syntax of young children are two of the leading examples. Seminars in English research methods have been held at national conventions of NCTE. The National Conference on Research in English cosponsors meetings at which certain aspects of writing are considered. An accounting of this increased attention to research in writing should now be attempted, including the composing process, handwriting, spelling, linguistic structures, and psycholinguistic growth and competency. Publications on children's writing appear to be increasing in number; they need to be analyzed to determine whether the appearance of improved research quality, as well as sheer frequency, is genuine and not illusory.

For all the apparent productiveness of the present decade in getting at the nature of the writing of children and adolescents, certain questions continue to be perplexing. What causes youngsters to want to write? How much motivation is inborn, is just because fundamentally we are communicating animals? How much stems from home, from contact with adults whom children see writing for obvious and satisfying purposes? How much motivation is affected by the media, those complex influences that touch us all? What fraction of motivation to write is built upon early approval at home, when a laborious "drawing" of words on paper extends the reach of young explorers to a realm they only vaguely sense? Does the desire to write need constant rekindling by peers and adults who give immediate approval to each effort to communicate on paper? What satisfactions are needed by adolescents to fortify their confidence and their urge to write? We teachers and researchers are only stumbling toward some answers to these questions.

And still more questions should be asked. How does stimulation to write differ from motivation? How are the two integrated into the affective-cognitive systems of the learner? When is requirement a constructive force? When is it helpful and when destructive? Can schools do anything to counter strongly negative parental influences, sometimes direct and forceful, sometimes covert but nonetheless powerful?

Much more also needs to be done in investigating the relation of writing to oral language. Beginnings we have, and they need to be built upon. How does the relative permanence of magnetic tape affect the need to write? The same kind of question needs to be pursued in considering the relation of oral language to reading. And further, is there a supporting relation between television and writing? If yes, under what conditions? Much more needs to be learned about the uses of the tape recorder as an aid to writing. Not only can syntax be investigated in studying this relationship, but it may also be possible to perceive some of the bridges from the unconscious to the conscious which may be the very essence of composing. Hard, yes, but vastly important! Fortunately there are some models that good researchers can replicate and adapt to special circumstances.

CURRENT TECHNIQUES IN EXAMINING COMPOSING PROCESSES

One way to economize research effort is to replicate outstanding or seminal studies. Only three such studies are reported here, much too briefly. The first is the doctoral study by Graves (1973) at the University of Buffalo, supervised by Walter Petty and included among those of "promising young researchers" cited by NCTE in 1974.

Graves's doctoral dissertation is a case study. It is, however, a case study with many ramifications, including well-nigh microscopic detail recorded as the subject, Michael, wrote. Graves reported the parents' reactions and general ideas about their son's schooling and home interests, along with observations of relationships with peers in school and with brother and sister at home.

Selecting Michael as the subject of the case study was, in itself, an unusual and productive technique. The purpose of the investigation was to study behaviors related to the writing process, to formulate instructional hypotheses, and to derive directions for further research in writing. Four second-grade classrooms in two public schools in a residential community near Buffalo, New York, furnished the subjects for observation: seven pupils, in addition to Michael, were studied with equal care but were minimally reported. Adult males in the community were largely blue-collar workers, and the number of school years completed by adults averaged 12.2; this parental background was typical for the children in the four second-grade classes. Two rooms were rated *formal;* two, *informal.* Classrooms were designated *formal* if thirty percent of each day's activities were chosen by the pupils; in *informal* classes, the pupils chose at least sixty percent of their activities. In the formal classes, no more than thirty percent of the teacher's time was spent with groups of fewer than five children, whereas, in the informal rooms, no less than sixty percent of her time was spent with groups of fewer than five pupils. The teachers were women, each with a minimum of six years of experience. Two children were chosen from each of the four classes; their mean age at the beginning of the study was 7.7 years. No children of unusually high intellectual capacity or who showed emotional or learning difficulties were included.

Data were collected from the first week of December 1972 to mid-April 1973. These data covered four phases of investigation: (1) logging of all writing by all pupils in the four classrooms, including later analysis for theme, length, illustrations, and teacher comments; (2) recording of behaviors during writing episodes; (3) recording of children's views of their own writing and of writing in general; and (4) completing of eight case studies, using material from parent interviews, tests, educational histories, and extended observations of each child.

The observation records of children's behaviors during writing episodes are in themselves worthy of much more extensive use in several types of research. Such details were recorded as the child's use of resources in the room for spelling or for information of various kinds; comments to peers, and whether such comments were initiated by the writer, a neighbor, or the teacher; proofreading, whether of a word just written or of the whole, so far as the writing had gone; and a host of other matters relevant to the actual committing of words to paper. Form and coding for this observation of behavior appear exemplary. All children in the four classes kept writing folders, in order to avoid excessive attention to the eight case-study children and to collect information about total classroom activity and atmosphere. In addition, the investigator noted the writing frequency of many children, the occurrence of assigned writing versus unassigned writing, the length of each piece, and the themes chosen by these seven-year-olds.

After the data were collected from the children and from the eight case-study pupils, Michael was chosen for elaborate reporting because a large proportion of his writing was unassigned. Graves assumed that such writing would reveal more about developmental phenomena. Michael had also shown a great amount of behavioral change during the four-month course of the study. The fifty-nine pages of his case study present a complex and illuminating picture of writing growth, both cognitive and effective. That these phenomena are observed within the comparatively short span of four and a half months presents some problems. Further studies need to examine a longer growth period.

The first two of Graves's conclusions about learning environments are given below.

> Informal environments give greater choice to children. When children are given choice to write, they write more and in greater length than when specific assignments are given.
>
> Results from informal environments demonstrate that children do not need direct motivation or supervision in order to write. (P. 211)

From Graves's seven conclusions on sex differences in writing, only three are quoted here.

> Girls compose longer writings than do boys in either formal or informal environments.
>
> Boys from either environment write more in unassigned writing than do girls. Unassigned writing seems to provide an incentive for boys to write about subjects not normally provided in teacher assigned work. Teachers do not normally assign work that includes themes from secondary and extended territory, the areas most used by boys in unassigned writing.
>
> Boys seldom use the first person form, especially the I form, unless they are developmentally advanced. (Pp. 211–12)

Important as are Graves's findings, his research techniques are perhaps more important. Among the procedures used, the case-study selection seems essential to the revelation of the uniqueness and complexity of the composing process. His delineation of the variables at work in any writing episode gives substance to the claim, usually based upon intuition and informal observation, that writing is indeed a many-faceted operation. Selection of individuals for special analysis, within the context of classroom procedures and with the climate and stimuli peculiar to each class, retained the natural setting so often omitted in research. Inclusion of parents through several interviews, informal yet disclosing matters germane to the children's growth, was of equal value.

Replication of Graves's study at later age levels and application of segments of it to other seven-year-olds seem to be obvious next steps to add to our knowledge about the nature of, and the relationships among, many variables in composing. One curious omission from the investigator's description of classroom stimuli was library use. Also omitted were descriptions of the sharing of literature in group activities or in individual conferences.

A study of the use of tape recorders as an adjunct to composing, specifically, to hear what one says as one thinks/writes, was reported by Tovatt and Miller (1967). Working with ninth graders in the laboratory school at Indiana State University at Muncie, Indiana, they had the fortunate arrangement of a classroom adjoining a workroom containing eighteen study carrels. A stratified sample of pupils was assigned to experimental and control groups, and an experienced and enthusiastic teacher was selected for each class. The experimental groups had the advantage of demonstrations of how teachers used the recorder in their own composing. The investigators gave a vivid description of one such demonstration, in which the teacher asked for suggestions from the "unit theme" and, after some consideration, selected a topic. Donning a headset and starting the recorder, he paused as he tried to get a flow of ideas, to catch a feeling for the sound and rhythm of beginning phrases, and then said the words as he put them on paper. He waited when necessary to let his pen catch up with his voice. After a paragraph or so, he played back what he had written, stopping at times to insert or to cross out words on his paper. He then pointed out to the class how he made certain choices, the point of view he wanted to establish for a particular audience, and other matters. He was frank about his groping tentativeness as he wrote and how he tested the effectiveness of his efforts. Other details about rewriting and changing are included in the report.

This study was carried on with ninth graders for three successive years, beginning in the academic year 1964–1965. Careful records of work and tests were analyzed with the following results: The first hypothesis was that students taught by the oral-aural-visual (OAV) procedure would achieve greater competence. The second hypothesis was that such students would develop a more favorable attitude toward writing. Analysis of test results and ratings of students' writings showed no significant superiority of either conventional or OAV approaches. However, gains made by OAV classes were markedly greater than were normative standards for the tests used. Nor did either group show a more positive attitude toward English, but it might be surmised that the generally higher achievement in reading, writing, talking, and listening indicates a more positive attitude. Although their results were inconclusive, these investigators used an approach well worth further trial, as is the examination of linkages between listening, writing, and talking. Teacher demonstration followed by self-analysis is a variable, of course, that should be accounted for in future studies.

A third research design deserving attention is that by Emig (1971). This study applied a case-study method to twelfth graders representing diverse social strata in the greater metropolitan area of Chicago. Eight students volunteered, five girls and three boys. Six were recommended by their high school English chair as "good" writers, and three were NCTE

Achievement Award winners. Each of the eight met four times with the investigator, the first time for an informal session followed by a short writing exercise. In this writing episode, each subject spoke aloud what he or she was thinking and writing. This oral production was tape recorded, and the investigator sat nearby so that she could observe and take notes. The sessions differed in the kind of writing asked for. Further, each student gave a writing "biography," revealing recollections of earlier writing experiences, whether encouraging or discouraging in effect. The students engaged in *reflexive* writing, defined as a contemplative extension of personal thought and feeling, and in *extensive* writing, defined as active, informative, and audience oriented. The latter was more often done for English class assignments in their respective schools.

Testing four hypotheses concerning high school students' composing processes revealed many findings and implications about the teaching of English, in counterpoint to the needs of students and the needs of society. What is of great significance in building future research is the application of case-study methods using students' oral verbalization of what they think and feel as they write. Refinements and extensions of this technique are potentially numerous. Emig was generous in her critique of the size and selectivity of her sample and other details of the investigation. The study furnished models for adaptation to younger students, as well as to adults, and shows ways of systematizing some aspects of recording and analyzing those recordings. Moreover, its presentation of writings about writing is itself a valuable demonstration of scholarship.

CONCLUSION

With some knowledge of historical trends in teaching and research and with models from recent investigations, researchers now have much to look forward to in pursuing the questions still unanswered. More precise research procedures and increased interest in composing processes of individual writers in their social settings auger well for the future.

REFERENCES

Basic Issues in the Teaching of English. From a series of conferences held throughout 1958. *English Journal* 48 (September 1959). [ED 016 640]

Bestor, A. *Educational Wastelands.* Urbana, Illinois: University of Illinois Press, 1953.

Braddock, Richard; Lloyd-Jones, R.; Schoer, L.; and others. *Research in Written Composition.* Champaign, Illinois: National Council of Teachers of English, 1963. [ED 003 374]

Burrows, Alvina T. *Teaching Composition.* What Research Says to the Teacher, no. 18. Washington: National Education Association and American Educational Research Association, 1963. [ED 017 482]

Burrows, Alvina T., chair; Parke, M. B.; Edmund, N. R.; DeBoer, J. J.; Horn, T. D.; Herrick, V. E.; and Strickland, R. G. *Children's Writing: Research in Composition and Related Skills.* National Conference on Research in English. Champaign, Illinois: National Council of Teachers of English, 1960—1961. [ED 090 546]

Davis, Emerson. *The Teacher Taught; or, The Principles and Modes of Teaching.* Boston: Marsh, Lyon, and Webb, 1839.

DeBoer, John J. "Composition, Handwriting and Spelling," *Review of Educational Research* 21 (April 1961): 161—72.

Dixon, John. *Growth through English.* London: Automatic Address Association, 1967. [ED 014 491]

Eliot, Charles W., chair. *Report of the Committee of Ten on Secondary School Studies With Reports of the Conferences Arranged by the Committee.* New York: American Book Co., 1894.

Emig, Janet. *The Composing Processes of Twelfth Graders.* Research Report, no. 13. Urbana, Illinois: National Council of Teachers of English, 1971. [ED 058 205]

Golub, Lester S. *Written Language Development and Instruction of Elementary School Children.* Paper presented to the National Conference on Research in English, National Council of Teachers of English convention, 1973. [ED 073 474]

Graves, Donald H. "Children's Writing: Research Directions and Hypotheses Based upon an Examination of the Writing Processes of Seven Year Old Children." Doctoral dissertation, State University of New York at Buffalo, 1973. [ED 095 586]

Hatfield, W. Wilbur. *An Experience Curriculum in English.* English Monograph, no. 4. New York: D. Appleton-Century Co., 1935.

Hinsdale, Burke A. *Teaching the Language-Arts: Speech, Reading, Composition.* New York: D. Appleton, 1898.

Hosic, James F., compiler. *Reorganization of English in Secondary Schools.* Department of the Interior, Bureau of Education, Bulletin, 1917, no. 2. Washington, D.C.: U.S. Government Printing Office, 1917. [ED 090 533]

Hunt, Kellogg W. *Grammatical Structures Written at Three Grade Levels.* Research Report, no. 3. Champaign, Illinois: National Council of Teachers of English, 1964. P. 49. [ED 113 735]

Kantor, Kenneth J. "Creative Expression in the English Curriculum." *Research in the Teaching of English* 9 (spring 1975): 5—29.

Loban, Walter D. *The Language of Elementary School Children.* Research Report, no. 1. Champaign, Illinois: National Council of Teachers of English, 1963. [ED 001 875]

Lundsteen, Sara, ed. *Help for the Teacher of Written Composition (K—9): New Directions in Research.* Urbana, Illinois: National Conference on Research in English and the ERIC Clearinghouse on Reading and Communication Skills, 1976. [ED 120 731]

Lynd, A. *Quackery in the Public Schools.* Boston: Little, Brown and Co., 1950.

Mearns, Hughes. *Creative Youth.* New York: Doubleday and Co., 1929.
———. *Creative Power: The Education of Youth in the Creative Arts.* 2nd rev. ed. Gloucester, Massachusetts: Peter Smith, 1975.

Mencken, H. L. *Happy Days, 1880—1892.* New York: Alfred A. Knopf, 1940. P. 33.
2nd rev. ed. Gloucester, Massachusetts: Peter Smith, 1975.

Muller, Herbert J. *The Uses of English: Guidelines for the Teaching of English from the Anglo-American Conference at Dartmouth College.* New York: Holt, Rinehart and Winston, 1967. [ED 014 492]

O'Donnell, Roy C.; Griffin, W. J.; and Norris, R. C. *Syntax of Kindergarten and Elementary School Children: A Transformational Analysis.* Research Report, no. 8. Champaign, Illinois: National Council of Teachers of English, 1967. [ED 070 093]

Smith, Dora V. *Class Size in High School English, Methods and Results.* Minnesota: University of Minnesota Press, 1931.

Strickland, Ruth G. "The Language of Elementary School Children: Its Relationship to the Language of Reading Textbooks and the Quality of Reading of Selected Children." *Bulletin of the School of Education, Indiana University* 38 (July 1962). [ED 002 970]

Tovatt, Anthony, and Miller, E. L. "The Sound of Writing." *Research in the Teaching of English* 1 (1967): 176—89.

Tway, Doris E. "A Study of the Feasibility of Training Teachers to Use the Literary Rating Scale in Evaluating Children's Fiction Writing." Doctoral dissertation, Syracuse University, 1971. [ED 053 139]

Reading Instruction and Research: In Historical Perspective

H. ALAN ROBINSON
Hofstra University

Burrow's trailblazing chapter on instruction and research in written composition stands as one of very few reviews with this historical focus. In contrast, this chapter represents, in the main, a synthesis of much that has already been written about reading instruction and research. Nila Banton Smith is thanked for furnishing the primary source on which the chapter is based. Only the part covering the period from 1965 to 1976 "originated" from the observations, insights, and educated guesses of this writer.

The sole method of teaching the reading of English in seventeenth century colonial America, to our knowledge, was "the ancient classical method of having the child start with a mastery of letters, then of syllables, and finally of words and sentences" (Mathews 1966, p. 27). Since that time, what I have chosen to call the *overlap principle* has been in evidence. Essentially, the overlap principle addresses itself to the repetition, through the centuries, of previously introduced methods that overlap (sometimes in small and often in large measure) those procedures introduced in a given era. Then the "new" methods take on the overlapping role as they remain, in varying degrees, across time. Today, as I believe I demonstrate later, we have vestiges of a number of the methods used at one time or another in the past.

The nature of the materials used as bases for the teaching of reading has changed more dramatically over time, although the overlap principle is discernible to some extent. The hornbook and the Psalter are museum pieces, but basal readers still flood the market, along with individual volumes aimed at improving reading ability. The content of the materials has met the needs of given epochs of our history; or, rather, the content has been structured to meet needs seen by authors and publishers.

It seems interesting to view the overlap principle in operation, as we trace both methods and materials across the unfolding of an independency of states to our present status as the United States. In the bulk of this chapter, I attempt to present a picture of historical trends in reading methodology, the content and structure of instructional and supplemental materials, and, to a limited extent, research activity.

In preparing the chapter, I utilized a number of primary and secondary sources—all of value. But, as indicated earlier, I leaned most heavily on Smith's intensive and extensive review, *American Reading Instruction*, published by the International Reading Association in 1965. In fact, this chapter is organized essentially in line with the time periods Smith used as her framework for looking at reading instruction from a historical perspective. For minutely detailed descriptions of methods and materials up to 1965, I recommend reading Smith's engaging and largely objective document on reading instruction in the United States.

BEFORE INDEPENDENCE

The first instructional materials used in reading (by English-speaking colonists) were imported from Great Britain. The materials emphasized religious content, and, almost always, at one point or another in the instructional sequence, the Psalter (a book of psalms used primarily for devotional purposes) and the Bible were in evidence.

For the very beginning stages of instruction, the hornbook, also imported from Great Britain, was frequently used. The hornbook was usually about three inches by four inches of paper fastened on a thin paddle-shaped piece of wood, iron, pewter, or even ivory or silver. At first the hornbook only contained the alphabet, but the content was soon expanded to include syllables and some basic religious selections. Smith (1965, p. 6) conjectured that a hornbook made of gingerbread, a favorite of the time, "was perhaps the first attempt to motivate reading instruction."

The ABC book was sometimes used following the completion of the hornbook, but most often the first book was called a primer, not because it was a *first* book, but because it was primary "in containing the 'minimum essentials' deemed necessary for one's spiritual existence" (Smith, p. 8). *The New England Psalter*, *The Protestant Tutor*, and *The New England Primer* were among the most popular texts of the day. Spellers were introduced, and, as Hodges described in chapter one, they added the dimension of spelling instruction but also included instruction in reading, religion, and morals. Strong's *England's Perfect School-Master* was one of the first spellers on the market—1710.

Usually the books were very small, often about two and a half inches by four and a half inches in size. Most of the instructional materials proceeded from simple to complex in respect to number of letters and syllables. No provision was made for repetition or distribution of the words being introduced. The rate of introduction of new words per page ranged from twenty to one hundred.

During this time period, no professional books, manuals, or courses of study existed to provide conceptual bases for the teaching of reading. Methods were imported (for English-speaking colonists) from Great Britain. The following sequence, apparently growing from a simplistic notion that instruction proceeds from small to large units, seemed to be the customary methodology.

1. Learn the alphabet by rote, forward and backward.
2. Point out the individual letters, in the alphabet and as they appear in words. (There appears to have been some use of squares of ivory with pictures and letters on them.)
3. After mastering all the letters, proceed to the syllabarium (organized groups of consonant-vowel clusters) and learn them by rote: *ba, be, bi, bo, bu*, and so on.
4. Then, using the ability to name the letters, spell out lists of short words—using this [magical] means of pronouncing the words.
5. Proceed to memorization of sentences and selections.
6. In some cases, answer general questions about selections.

In all cases, content was considered more important than any methodology directed toward developing independent readers. Oral reading was promoted as *the* reading procedure for social and religious needs. *The reader in the family read to other family members from what was probably the one piece of reading material in the home—the Bible.

1776 TO 1840

Not surprisingly, the emphasis in the content of instructional reading materials from 1776 to 1840 was nationalistic, with a good deal of the moralistic included. (There was overlap, of course, for many of the materials used prior to independence were still in service.) Led by Noah Webster with his blue-back spellers in a variety of editions, authors aimed to purify the language in the U.S., to develop loyalty to the new country, to inculcate high ideals of virtue and moral behavior, and to develop elocutionary ability. Hence, exercises focused on the *right* pronunciation, on patriotic and historical selections, proverbs, moral stories, fables, and so forth, as well as on expressive oral reading. Expository literature dominated the scene, however. Numerous new authors produced popular primers, readers, and spellers. Also the first *set* of readers was born.

The "spelling" method of teaching reading was still prevalent, but, with Webster and others attempting to unify the language, a type of phonics was developed. Sounds were taught, letter by letter and syllable by syllable, to stress articulation and pronunciation, as well as to "correct" dialects. Worcester, Gallaudet, and Taylor, in the period between 1820 and 1835, advocated a word method which sustained some popularity. Gallaudet introduced the word-to-letter method, in which a word was shown under the picture of a particular object—the beginnings of developing a sight vocabulary; however, at that time, pupils learned each of the letters in the word.

Nevertheless, whatever method was used to try to learn words, the overriding emphasis appeared to be on elocution. The teacher would read a sentence, and the pupils would keep pronouncing it until they said it "properly." This approach necessitated learning much information about commas, colons, and other punctuation and about the rules of reading aloud.

During the latter part of this time period, Keagy, a physician, introduced *The Pestalozzian Primer*, with emphasis on meaning and thinking. Interpreting Pestalozzi, Keagy spoke out against saying words "without having the corresponding ideas awakened in their [the youngsters'] minds" (Mathews 1966, p. 65). He suggested that children be helped to build up much useful knowledge prior to reading and that they then start reading whole words at sight. He felt that word analysis should follow fluent reading of stories. Keagy appears to have been a minority forerunner of the greater emphasis on thinking during reading which emerged as one definite trend in the next time period.

1840 TO 1880

This time period was characterized, according to Smith, by a search for more effective methods of teaching reading, since the national emphasis appeared to focus on promoting intelligent citizenship—not an unexpected trend for a developing nation. The content of readers was turning from patriotic and moral selections (at a slow but steady pace) to emphasis on reading for information, reading to find out about real events, and reading to learn more about nature. Some literary selections were included mainly for elocutionary purposes. Often the content seemed dull, particularly in the beginning books of the extremely popular McGuffey readers. In these beginning books, sentences were emphasized, rather than longer selections; the sentences were usually quite meaningless and uninteresting, as they were "subservient to the phonetic elements which McGuffey selected for drill purposes" (Smith, p. 106). One set of readers, by Willson, featured only scientific content.

During this period, though, another way of approaching reading instruction began to bloom. Although Keagy's *The Pestalozzian Primer*, introduced during the preceding time period (1776 to 1840), had some influence and popularity, it remained for Horace Mann to really guide Pestalozzian principles and methods into American reading instruction. Mann provided the developing discipline of reading instruction with its first conceptual framework. He denounced most existing methods as refusing children a chance to think; he said that they were so imitative that "a parrot or even an idiot could do the same thing" (Smith, p. 78). The Pestalozzian movement, which stressed use of all senses and immediate application to meaningful situations, resulted in the use of word methods, pictures, and materials dealing with objects and experiences familiar to children.

Word methods appeared to grow out of the application of Pestalozzian principles, but also out of the independent thinking of individuals who rebelled against what they considered to be boring methodology that interfered with learning. Bumstead, who based his *My Little Primer* specifically on a word method, stated that "children are delighted with ideas; and in school exercises . . . they are disgusted with their absence." He also indicated that the words in his readers were chosen regardless of length and "the popular opinion that a word is *easy* because it is *short*." He said a word "is easy or difficult, chiefly, as it expresses an idea easy or difficult of comprehension" (Smith, p. 88).

Word methods, however, did not concentrate on context. Pupils were first confronted with lists of words and then went on to the approaches still used most frequently—the "alphabet-phonetic" methods. The syllabarium method disappeared, but "heightened attention to the principle of 'proceeding from the simple to the complex' was generally and painstakingly applied" (Smith, p. 86). Spelling and reading instruction were closely tied together essentially through concentration on phonetics, or phonics.

At the same time, emphasis was still placed on expressive oral reading and elocutionary ability, in company with many of the overlapping aims of the earlier periods. Nevertheless, the introduction of some stress on meaning was prevalent both in the discussions of individual words and when pupils read passages. "Some attention was now called to meanings in the upper grades through questions on the content and definitions of words, both of which were specified in the book" (Smith, p. 86).

Because of the development of graded schools during this time period (a Pestalozzian influence), graded reading series were introduced, edited by such contemporary educators as McGuffey, Tower, Hillard, and Bumstead. (The McGuffey readers remained the most popular, even into the next era.) The books themselves were longer and narrower than those of the past. Fewer words were introduced in the primers than before, and they were repeated often during the series. Some of the series included instructions to the teacher at the beginning of individual volumes. No teacher's manuals and few professional books were yet introduced. A few meager courses of study existed in some school systems.

1880 TO 1910

Smith named this the period of "reading as a cultural asset," for there was a distinctive trend for a stabilizing nation to turn toward the cultivation of taste in literature. Herbart's doctrines centering on reading to discover the truth and on enjoying characters and plots were becoming popular in the United States. Charles W. Eliot, then president of Harvard, advocated the abolishment of basal readers and suggested substituting original literary works in their place.

A few professional books and articles were published during this time period. The most noteworthy book was written by Huey (1908); it is considered the first scientific contribution to reading instruction. This volume was reprinted quite recently (1968), not just for its historical value but because many of the ideas and problems discussed by Huey are even more pertinent today than they were earlier. Full-fledged courses of study also emerged on the educational scene, and many contained pages devoted to reading instruction. A few separate courses of study were focused on reading.

Although basal readers still flourished, supplemental materials were introduced to balance the reading diet. Smith (p. 125) quoted from a contemporary article which clarified the trend.

> Now it is very evident that the advantages which the readers have as exercises in elocution and drill-books prevent them in most cases from inspiring any love of good reading and from giving the power of sustained interest. It is to promote these two objects that supplemental reading has been introduced into many of our schools. Books and magazines are brought forward to do what the reading books from their nature cannot do.

A number of methods were in use during this period, although the alphabet method seems to have died. Phonics, or phonetics, was in wide use, although there were loud voices raised against an overdose of phonics, since there appeared to be many poor readers in the upper grades who had been raised on strong phonics programs. Nevertheless, major emphasis on sound/symbol relationships flourished as *the* approach to learning how to read. Pollard's synthetic method of 1889, with its intense stress on phonics, was popular; on the other hand, Pollard did give careful consideration to children's interests and attempted to make readings and exercises interesting.

At this time, two short-lived, contrived alphabetic-phonetic systems were introduced. The "scientific alphabet," used in the first reader of the Standard Reading Series published in 1902, "reduced the number of characters needed in representing the sounds in the English language by respelling words and by omitting silent letters. Some diacritical markings also appeared in this alphabet" (Smith, p. 127). In the "Shearer system" published in 1894, "a letter's sound where it might be equivocal is represented by a mark which constantly stands for that sound, and for that sound only, irrespective of what the letter may be. Comparatively few marks are needed and the constant value of the marks is supposed to give an easy guide to pronunciation. The silent letters are indicated by a dot" (Smith, p. 128).

Several basal readers introduced the word method during this period. Phonics was used after a stock of sight words had been developed. Outgrowths of the word method, sentence and story methods focused on familiarization or memorization of the larger language units before working on specific word-attack techniques, essentially phonics.

The instructional materials themselves, both basal and supplementary, were more attractive than in past periods. Cloth covers replaced cardboard covers, type became clearer and larger, volumes were closer in size to present-day books, and colored pictures, although sparse, were introduced.

Concern for children who were having problems learning to read and the ever-broadening significance of reading in daily life in the United States apparently were major factors in the burgeoning of research during this chronological period. Although most of the studies were laboratory-type studies and had little impact on the classroom, these initial investigators called attention to, and began to contribute insights into, such factors as "rate in reading, distinctions between silent and oral reading, and individual differences in reading" (Smith, p. 155).

1910 TO 1925

This period in reading history was called the "scientific movement" by Smith, for it marked the advent of instruments of measurement. The Gray Standardized Oral Reading Paragraphs, published in 1915, were soon followed by a number of other reading tests, mainly tests of silent reading. In addition, much more emphasis than ever before was placed on reading research.

A true innovation, unaffected by the overlap principle, emerged—emphasis on silent reading. The rather rapid change from stress on oral reading to the vigorous teaching of silent reading was probably related to several factors. There were increasing demands placed on reading for meaning, instead of on oral exercise, in order to meet the varied needs of society. There were loud cries for improving reading instruction, for it had been found during the war years "that thousands of our soldiers could not read well enough to follow printed instructions used in connection with military life" (Smith, p. 158). Research reports began to show the superiority of silent reading over oral reading for both fluency and comprehension. Contemporary writers urged that schools place emphasis on the teaching of silent reading. Finally, the birth of standardized silent reading tests called for appropriate shifts in teaching methodology.

Although the number of professional texts was small, there were numerous professional articles; both texts and articles focused largely on silent reading. The most popular professional text continued to be Huey's *The Psychology and Pedagogy of Reading*, revised in 1912 and again in 1915. Many courses of study appeared as part of an English or overall curriculum guide. A few cities published separate reading guides. There was a proliferation of manuals, both revisions of old ones and some brand new, accompanying basal programs. The manuals were particularly directed toward the teaching of silent reading. There was usually at least one paper-covered manual for each grade.

The basal readers themselves centered on factual, informative material. According to the authors of a widely used basal series of the time,

> to feed the child on an exclusive literary diet that is entirely divorced from the actual situations in the world in which he lives, will defeat one of the fundamental purposes of teaching reading. A certain amount of fanciful material may be legitimate. But at the present time the supply of "Little Red Hen" and "Gingerbread Boy" type of material, largely used in the schools, needs to be supplemented by a suitable proportion of factual material, in order that the child's thinking may be more directly related to the actual experiences which he daily encounters. (Smith, p. 173)

There was an abundance of supplemental materials of all kinds. Since emphasis was placed on silent reading, numerous aids were directed toward helping teachers cope with "seatwork" problems. Flash cards and other devices which could be used independently were prevalent. Pupils were asked to answer objective-type questions—often in written form—about selections in both supplemental and basal programs.

Methods were aimed at improvement of comprehension. Lessons often began at the sentence level, through directions for reading presented orally or on the chalkboard. Children then read silently to find specific answers to questions or to interpret a passage. Some emphasis was placed on speed of reading. Phonics, or phonetics, was still taught in the primary grades as a separate group of lessons. Experience charts were used, to a limited extent, in limited fashion.

During the preceding period, from 1880 to 1910, it had been discovered that many intermediate children were unable to read well. During this period (1910 to 1925) discovery continued, and the first vague beginnings of special help for poor readers became visible. Also, there seemed to be more general concern than ever before for attending to individual differences.

1925 TO 1935

Although this period was a brief one in the history of United States reading instruction, it was aptly named by Smith the period of "intensive research and application." Two differing philosophies of reading instruction emerged from the roots developed in earlier periods: (1) There is a sequence of skills to be learned by all children, and these can be plotted out in a basic program by authoritative adults. (2) The reading needs of children can best be met through their reasoning processes as they carry out their own purposes and solve their own problems (the activity movement).

Reading researchers were remarkably prolific during this time period, and the quality of the research was constantly improving. Although researchers focused on many aspects of reading, reading interests, reading disability, and readiness for beginning reading were the topics most frequently studied. Although there was continued interest during the early part of this period in studying silent reading, few researchers seem to have remained interested by the close of the period.

Most reading programs attempted to adhere to an influential set of objectives published in *The Twenty-Fourth Yearbook of the National Society for the Study of Education*, Part 1 (1925). These objectives focused on enabling the reader:

> To participate intelligently in the thought life of the world and appreciatively in its recreational activities (p. 9)
>
> To develop strong motives for, and permanent interests in reading that will inspire the present and future life of the reader and provide for the wholesome use of leisure time (p. 11)
>
> To develop the attitudes, habits, and skills that are essential in the various types of reading activities in which children and adults should engage (p. 12)

Many of the professional books and courses of study published during this short time period were devoted to reading. Some courses of study dealt with specific aspects of reading—remedial reading, reading factual material, audience reading, recreational reading, vocabulary development; two were devoted to the reading of mathematics. Manuals accompanying basal readers became much like professional books, were less dogmatic than in the past, contained more optional activities, and suggested many supplementary activities.

Varied instructional materials were used in both "sequence-of-skills" and "activity" programs. Abundant and beautiful supplemental materials were available. Most of the stories in supplemental materials were realistic; few folk tales and fanciful tales were published. Some sets of supplemental materials emerged.

Readers, of course, were the foundation of the sequence-of-skills programs. The preprimer was introduced as readiness for the primer. The books were much more attractive and colorful than in the past. Care was exercised to introduce only words used most frequently according to vocabulary lists; some attention was also paid to reducing the number of words in the early books. Words were repeated often so learners might remember them. Sets of readers were available mainly through the intermediate grades, although one set went to grade seven and another to grade eight. William S. Gray and Arthur I. Gates were prominent developers of basal series.

Reading instruction was generally conducted throughout the school day and not just during a reading period. In most programs, the basal was used daily as the main feature of the reading program. A correlation approach was also in use—if reading a unit on Japan in a basal, pupils would also study Japan in geography, work arithmetic problems about Japan, and so on. Some educators appeared to be reaching toward an integration approach (reading not taught as a separate subject but used as a tool in all subjects), but the result was most often correlation.

Specific methods were varied. All manuals dealt with phonics in some way. Gates developed his "intrinsic" method: word-recognition techniques (including context clues) were to be part of, and not apart from, silent reading exercises. In some programs, phonics was taught only to those who needed it. In other cases, phonics was delayed until children were able to note similarities and differences in words. In sequence-of-skills programs, developmental lessons were planned dealing with specific skills. Exercises provided for both work-type and recreational reading.

Much attention was given to the concept of individual needs. In sequence-of-skills programs, the three-group method was most often employed as a means of providing for individual needs. In the activity movement, the program was organized around the needs and activities of children, through a variety of themes. Some of the activity programs dispensed with basal readers.

Diagnosis and remediation was a chief topic of study during this period. Most manuals of basal series discussed techniques for helping disabled readers. The Fernald technique, introduced in the preceding period, was beginning to be used, particularly by some clinical psychologists. Psychological and educational clinics came into being with primary concentration on diagnosis rather than remediation.

This time period saw the birth of the term "reading readiness," nurtured by Rousseau, Pestalozzi, Froebel, and Herbart, and now crystallized by Dewey. The readiness period for reading was both discussed and recommended in *The Twenty-Fourth Yearbook of the National Society for the Study of Education*, Part 1 (1925). Also, the results of a doctoral study by Reed (1927) demonstrated "that one in every six children failed at the end of the first semester in first grade, and that one in every eight failed at the end of the second semester in first grade" (Smith, p. 261). Reed's results appeared to strengthen the growing awareness of a need for focusing attention on reading readiness.

1935 TO 1950

During this fifteen-year span, appropriately named "the period of international conflict" by Smith, emphasis was placed on systematic reading instruction and on reading in contemporary life. A host of materials was published that centered on high school, college, and adult reading as outgrowths of the realization (first arrived at during World War I) that young people entering the armed forces could not read well enough to cope with their duties. Developmental reading programs were instituted in high schools and colleges, with emphasis on reading in content areas.

A number of important professional books were published, and their far-reaching influence may be felt even today: Gates, *The Improvement of*

Reading; Betts, *Foundations of Reading Instruction;* Monroe, *Children Who Cannot Read;* Fernald, *Remedial Techniques in Basic School Subjects;* and Helen M. Robinson, *Why Pupils Fail in Reading.* Some of the professional texts were general in nature, but a number concentrated on specific aspects. In fact, the first volumes on secondary school reading were published at this time. Manuals accompanying basals, as well as supplementary materials, were very thorough in nature.

The few new series introduced during this period had reading-readiness books preceding preprimers. There were generally two books per grade, from second grade on. A continued reduction in the total number of words introduced and in the number of words per page was evident. Repetitions of words were better controlled. The stories were predominantly realistic and informative, with a scattering of the fanciful. There tended to be more interrelationship with the other language arts and, in one series, overall emphasis on social studies and science. Reading readiness began to be recognized as an important concept at all levels of instruction.

Long, carefully organized skill charts accompanied basals, and word recognition was broken down into phonics, structural analysis, and context clues. Phonics instruction in grade one was generally limited. Work-type reading was now called work study or study skills and generally was broken down into information locating, evaluation, organization, and retention. Comprehension was segmented in a variety of ways but most often in these general categories: simple comprehension, higher mental processes, and critical thinking or critical reading. Some attention was given speed of reading and skimming.

Attention to individual needs remained a viable concept. Grouping was the main approach to caring for individual needs, and the objective of flexibility was more discussed than achieved.

A great deal of emphasis was placed on remediation, and reading clinics developed at a rapid pace. A number of instruments were invented or adapted for use in diagnosis and instruction: telebinocular, ophthalmograph, metronoscope, tachistoscopes, Harvard Films, and others.

1950 TO 1965

Smith called the period from 1950 to 1965 a time of "expanding knowledge and technological revolution." During these fifteen years, many professional books were published. New and revised basals with extensive manuals spanned the elementary grades, sometimes covering grades seven and eight. Stories were mostly realistic. The average number of words introduced in basals was still decreasing. Repetitions of vocabulary words usually were carefully controlled. The civil rights movement raised the moral and economic consciousness of authors and publishers; multicultural readers and supplementary materials were produced. At first the materials were quick responses to a need—change the pictures, alter some stereotypes. By the end of this time period, these materials had improved in quality and in response to at least some of the needs of some of the learners.

At the same time, multiple texts were being introduced into classes, in order to care for individual needs. Individualized reading programs and individualized instruction, visible throughout our history, now emerged with a sound conceptual base partly due to Olson's ideas of "seeking, self-selection, and pacing." The concept of individualized reading was used in collaboration with basal instruction by some teachers, but, in a large number of situations, individualized reading programs replaced basal programs. Programmed reading, with or without hardware, was introduced as part of the concept of individualized instruction; unfortunately, most of the programs concentrated on "pacing" rather than on overall individualization.

Reading-readiness programs were evident, but criticism, particularly of the instructional materials and activities, was growing. Questions were asked, not necessarily about the concept, but rather about the procedures used to develop this readiness. During this time, in some situations, a child could be held back to complete the parts of the structured readiness program, even though he or she was ready, or even able, to read.

Linguists became insterested in reading instruction, and "linguistic" readers came into being. Materials were usually based on the gradual introduction of word or spelling patterns, although some attention was focused on sentence patterns. Pitman's initial teaching alphabet (i.t.a.) found its way to this country in a set of materials prepared by Mazurkiewicz and Tanyzer in 1963 and 1964. Other augmented alphabets were tried, but none became as popular as i.t.a.

Essentially, however, instruction incorporated all of the reading skills discovered or developed over the years. All types of word-recognition clues were taught, and phonics, contrary to some notions, never left the basal programs. However, several critics claimed that phonics needed more emphasis (a recurring theme) and, as usual, publishers responded with renewed vigor. Austin and Morrison (1963), in their extensive study of elementary reading, observed that phonics was taught across the nation, often, in their view, at the expense of other learning.

Much stress appeared to be placed on the higher-level reading skills, such as critical reading, although Austin and Morrison found that such skills were discussed by educators more often than they were actually taught. Vocabulary and study-skills instruction seemed universal.

From 1960 on, there was a decided expansion of developmental reading programs in high schools, and many programs, most often of a corrective nature, were organized in colleges. Adult reading programs, for those functionally illiterate, as well as for those who could read well but who wanted to read better, became popular and were offered in adult education centers, as well as in libraries and in business settings. Clinics, private and public, developed at a fast pace to care for the needs of retarded readers in a society where high-level literacy seemed essential.

Research was prolific and improved in design. An increasing number of investigators became interested in the sociology of reading, although studies concentrating on psychological factors in reading also continued to be prominent. Doctoral dissertations were plentiful, and some of those student researchers may be credited with a movement toward looking intensively at the reading processes rather than stressing, as did so many researchers, evaluation of the products of reading or reading instruction (in essence, the test results).

1965 TO 1976

The time period from 1965 to 1976 is too close to the time of publication of this volume to allow us to stand back and look at the decade very objectively or, indeed, to give it a name. At this time, in the view of this writer, the decade in some ways seems to have been almost two separate periods, educationally speaking—the first half, one of hope and abundance; the second half, one of uncertainty and poverty. Certainly the total decade was characterized by overlapping methodologies resulting, as usual, in dichotomous suggestions, procedures, and instructional materials. Reading instruction encompassed emphases on phonics, context clues, content areas, rates of reading, study skills, reasoning, critical reading, and so on. Almost all of the approaches (in modern dress) utilized in the United States since 1840 were visible during this decade. The cry for more phonics issued loud and clear once again as *the* way of solving "the reading problem." And this in spite of a large-scale national study, described by Bond and Dykstra (1967), in which a major conclusion appeared to be that the teacher and the elements in the learning situation were more important than was any single method.

Particularly during the first half of the decade, when funds were available from many sources, authors and publishers answered the demands for many methods and for a multitude of materials. Books, workbooks, instruments, and computers abounded, offering schools a wide choice for their particular needs. Emphasis was placed on helping minority groups, and funds were available for additional personnel in the school system. The demand for reading teachers and the number in training were at all-time highs. The concept of accountability entered the educational arena. For a short time, schools bought programs on trial (payment dependent upon student achievement), and teachers often were judged on the ability of their students to achieve high scores.

During the latter part of the decade, inflation and recession succeeded in restricting budgets, and schools became more selective about their purchases. In addition, publishers had to evaluate the projects they planned to publish or revise. The educational scene reflected a new phenomenon: aside from the influence of lowered budgets, school populations—mainly in suburban areas—diminished as a result of "no growth" and the lowered national birthrate. A number of schools were closed, and thousands of teachers were excised. Although the national concern for eliminating illiteracy by 1980 received priority, numerous factors—even with the valiant efforts of the Right to Read Program—made it sound like "the impossible dream."

During the 1965—1976 period, particularly during the last five years, growing emphasis was placed on communication skills (including reading) that would help learners cope with the tasks confronting them in their everyday lives. Adult education programs began to focus on consumer education, health, job-finding skills, and ecology. In this amazingly complex and ever-changing society, it seems likely that coping skills will receive much more attention in the next decade, for younger learners as well as for adults.

In the opinion of this writer the most significant "innovation" during this decade, and slightly before, was the contribution to reading instruction made by linguistics, psycholinguistics, and sociolinguistics. There is still much to be learned, but I see promising signs of improved reading instruction as a result of increasing knowledge. Strickland (1962) should be thanked for pressuring the profession into looking at written language as it is processed by readers, in terms of syntax rather than just in terms of word difficulty and sentence length. Her study was followed rapidly by other researchers (including Loban 1963—1967; Ruddell 1963; Hunt 1965; O'Donnell, Griffin, and Norris 1967; Goodman 1964—1973; Peltz 1972) who made us realize how much we need to know about learners and their languages if we are to try to facilitate reading achievement. Young (1973), in a doctoral dissertation, critically reviewed and summarized studies concerned with the relationship of reading and linguistics.

CONCLUSION

Enlightened attitudes toward language usage and dialects, in my opinion, have been, and will continue to be, strong influences for improvement in reading instruction. The promising trend and the hope for the future was summed up well by Gunderson (1971):

> A teacher who has an understanding of language and its structure, and who possesses the requisite skills to understand and to capitalize on a child's particular strengths should be able to provide the proper opportunity for children to learn to read.

REFERENCES

Austin, Mary C., and Morrison, Coleman. *The First R.* New York: Macmillan Co., 1963.

Bond, Guy L., and Dykstra, Robert. "The Cooperative Research Program in First-Grade Reading Instruction." *Reading Research Quarterly* 2 (summer 1967): 1—142. [ED 014 417]

Goodman, Kenneth S. "A Linguistic Study of Cues and Miscues in Reading." 1964. [ED 015 087]

_____. "Study of Children's Behavior While Reading Orally." 1964. [ED 021 698]

_____. *Theoretically Based Studies of Patterns of Miscues in Oral Reading Performance.* Washington: Bureau of Research, Office of Education, April 1973. [ED 079 708]

Gunderson, Doris V. "Reading: The Past Revisited." November 1971. [ED 085 680]

Huey, Edmund B. *The Psychology and Pedagogy of Reading.* 1908. Reprint. Cambridge, Massachusetts: MIT Press, 1968.

Hunt, Kellogg W. *Grammatical Structures Written at Three Grade Levels.* Research Report, no. 3. Champaign, Illinois: National Council of Teachers of English, 1965. [ED 113 735]

Loban, Walter. *The Language of Elementary School Children.* Research Report, no. 1. Champaign, Illinois: National Council of Teachers of English, 1963. [ED 001 875]

_____. "Language Ability: Grades Seven, Eight, and Nine." Cooperative Research Project, no. 1131. Berkeley, California: University of California, 1964. [ED 001 275]

_____. "Language Ability: Grades Ten, Eleven, and Twelve." Berkeley, California: University of California, 1967. [ED 014 477]

Mathews, Mitford M. *Teaching to Read: Historically Considered.* Chicago: University of Chicago Press, 1966. [ED 117 649]

O'Donnell, Roy C.; Griffin, W. J.; and Norris, R. C. *Syntax of Kindergarten and Elementary School Children: A Transformational Analysis.* Research Report, no. 8. Champaign, Illinois: National Council of Teachers of English, 1967. [ED 070 093]

Olson, Willard. "Seeking, Self-Selection and Pacing in the Use of Books by Children." *The Packet* (spring 1962): 3—10.

Peltz, Fillmore K. "The Effect upon Comprehension of Repatterning Materials Based on Students' Writing Patterns." *Reading Research Quarterly* 9 (1973—1974): 603—21. [ED 086 990]

Reed, Mary M. "An Investigation of the Practice for the Admission of Children and the Promotion of Children from First Grade." Doctoral dissertation, Teachers College, Columbia University, 1927.

Ruddell, Robert B. "An Investigation of the Effect of the Similarity of Oral and Written Patterns of Language Structure on Reading Comprehension." Doctoral dissertation, Indiana University, 1963.

Smith, Nila Banton. *American Reading Instruction.* rev. ed. Newark, Delaware: International Reading Association, 1965.

Strickland, Ruth G. "The Language of Elementary School Children: Its Relationship to the Language of Reading Textbooks and the Quality of Reading of Selected Children." *Bulletin of the School of Education, Indiana University* 38 (July 1962). [ED 002 970]

Twenty-Fourth Yearbook of the National Society of the Study of Education. Part 1. Bloomington, Illinois: Public School Publishing Co., 1925.

Young, Sherrye L. S. "The Relationship of Reading and Linguistics: A Critical Essay and Annotated Bibliography." Doctoral dissertation, Ohio University, 1973.

Two Significant Trends in Reading Research

SAMUEL WEINTRAUB
State University of New York at Buffalo

In the preceding chapter, Robinson dealt essentially with reading instruction but also highlighted the research trends. It is obvious that he could not "cover" the history of reading research in great detail, for over nine thousand reading-research reports have been identified since William S. Gray first began in 1925 the publication of the annual summary of research in reading. Gray's reports encompass a wide range of topics and disciplines, as even the most cursory skimming of the subtopics in the summaries would indicate. The disciplines represented include sociology, psychology, optometry, neurology, psycholinguistics, journalism, and the fine arts. The very breadth of the disciplines included points out the diverse dimensions of the reading field.

Because of the complexity of the field and the sheer number of research reports available, it would be impossible to summarize the research trends in any organized, meaningful pattern. Even within any one of the three major subdivisions—sociology, psychology, and pedagogy—a great diversity can be identified. Incorporated within psychology of reading, for example, would be such topics as reading interests, learning, sociocultural influences, reading disability, modes of learning, sex differences, visual perception, language abilities, personality, and readability. Not only does each major category have its own trends, techniques, and unique historical development, but even within subcategories may be found unique types of research tools and techniques. The investigators within an area appear to be interested in pursuing an individualistic pattern that may have no bearing on, or even similarity to, any other area in reading, in terms of the tools and approaches utilized.

The very complexity of the field as a whole thus defies a logical, progressive historical treatment of the research therein. Therefore, in addition to Robinson's succinct overview, I have decided to focus on two research areas that can be traced back for about a century and that still command considerable interest among reading researchers. In fact, the first area discussed has been a major concern of teachers also, at a variety of instructional levels. The two areas contrast with one another on several counts: in concept, in the research tools used in each, and in the backgrounds of the researchers in each. In one area essentially the same types of tools have been used, with some advance in design sophistication, while in the other technological advances have made inroads into the types of techniques used. The areas—children's reading preferences or interests and eye movements during reading—have attracted researchers with quite different backgrounds; the differences may be partially responsible for the directions in which each area has progressed.

The remainder of this chapter is devoted to tracing the historical developments in each field and then comparing the two in terms of techniques employed, conceptual framework used, and researchers attracted.

RESEARCH IN CHILDREN'S READING INTERESTS

Perhaps the first published report on reading interests was that by True (1889). True kept track of the dates when new books were received in the school library and reported the number of times that they were checked out. True cautioned the reader that the record consisted only of books used out of school and, indeed, went on to state that no record had been made of the books' actual use but only of the fact that they had been checked out. He did not analyze the data in any manner but merely presented the data and permitted the reader to draw conclusions at will.

A number of techniques have been used to collect information about the reading interests of children. True's technique, with minor variations and especially with some modification in the area of analysis, is still being used. Larger studies of library usage continue to be reported; their level of sophistication varies. Other techniques used have included written logs, diaries, and inventories; individual structured interviews; forced-choice questionnaires, as well as other forced-choice situations; and solicitation of children's reactions to selections read to them.

Although it followed True's report by more than thirty-five years, the study by Terman and Lima (1925) was one of the earlier studies reported on children's reading interests, and it exemplified many of the techniques still in use. In this study, data were obtained from three sources —home, school, and children themselves. Nearly two thousand children were asked to keep a record of the books they read during a two-month period. Children were also asked to fill out an interest blank, on which they checked categories of stories that they liked to read. In addition, they were asked to list the four or five most enjoyable books that they had read during the past year.

Perhaps because of the size of the sample, because of its relatively early appearance in the literature, because of the prominence of Terman, or possibly due to the fact that the study appeared in book form rather than as a short journal article, the techniques used in this study seem to have influenced numerous researchers.

The question of the reliability of the records maintained by their subjects was acknowledged and briefly discussed by Terman and Lima. They indicated that they had received letters from a number of parents, stating either that the children had not read as much as they usually did or that the quality of the material read was not up to their children's usual standards. This information led Terman and Lima to believe that their data were as reliable as information of this sort could be and were not inflated by materials which had not been read.

Data collected by means of logs or records have an inherent danger, that the subject may overreport. Even researchers into the reading habits of adults recognize that this factor is at work. Depending on how the record is presented to them, subjects may be stimulated to read more than they might ordinarily do or, at least, to report reading even when they have not, in fact, done any. Rarely has the validity of such data been checked. One method would be to follow the children carefully, maintaining anecdotal information, to check library records, and even to query the subjects about the books they report having read. Only a selected sample would need to be followed in this way, but the information gained would indicate how much faith to put in the accuracy of the findings.

The interest inventory used by Terman and Lima is a fairly common type of data-gathering instrument today. The use of such instruments has flawed the research to date. Terman and Lima, for example, have no listing for animal stories. Supposedly, such books would fall under their categories "adventure stories," "nature study," or perhaps "stories of home life." Some investigators have used different categories to collect their data. Still others have used the same category titles but have varied their definitions of them. This lack of consistency in the development of techniques and instruments has resulted in an inability to meaningfully synthesize the knowledge base in this area. In addition, it has opened up the area to serious criticism, much of which has yet to be answered in any satisfactory manner.

The third type of information Terman and Lima collected from children, the listing of titles of books read within a given period of time, is also still in use, and it is subject to many of the same criticisms to which the previously mentioned two data-collecting devices are subject. First, the validity of such data is rarely established. Second, the titles that are collected in such reports are often categorized in different ways by different researchers—thereby creating difficulties for anyone attempting to summarize the research. The lack of rigor in defining categories and terms is a problem prevalent throughout the history of reading research generally, and this lack continues into the present.

The magnitude of the sample investigated by Norvell (1950) is one of the factors that has led to the importance of this study in any reference to research in the area of children's reading interests. Data were collected from some fifty thousand subjects in grades seven through twelve. The study provided an interest score for some seventeen hundred selections commonly used for study in English classes. Although previous studies had also determined interest scores for given titles, no one had set such a criterion as a minimum of three hundred student reports for establishing a score, nor had any other study used such a large population. Students were asked to indicate the title and author of a given selection and then to rate it on a three-point scale, from *very interesting* to *uninteresting*. The interest score was then based on a tabulation of these responses, and the composite ratings were presented to be used as guides in selecting materials. Although some attempt was made to establish the reliability of the subjects' reports, it still remains in some doubt. In addition, the limitations placed on the materials which could be reacted to, as well as the limitations of the instrument itself, all render the findings derived from such data somewhat questionable. The technique is not widely represented in the current research literature on reading interests, although variations and adaptations of it can be found. Generally, the users of the technique have not made as thorough an effort to establish the reliability of their instrument as Norvell did.

Another technique used involves a forced choice of fiction titles or categories. Generally, children are asked which of two or three titles they would most prefer to read. The problems with this approach, as well as with others, have been pointed out by Robinson and Weintraub (1973). In brief, the flaw in a forced-choice technique is that it is possible that none of the choices may be of interest. The findings of such a technique may reflect, then, choices made among topics of which all have little appeal.

Perhaps one of the more promising techniques used to collect data about children's reading interests has been the intensive individual interview. Stanchfield (1962) reported the use of this procedure. It is regrettable that no details were furnished about procedures used or questions asked. It is therefore impossible to evaluate the accuracy of the findings or to replicate the study with another population.

Wragg (1968) had pupils maintain a diary of what they had read for a week. The accuracy of such records needs to be carefully ascertained. In addition, the season of the year may have a significant effect on both the quantity and the type of literature read.

One other problem has been prevalent in the area of reading interests. Few reports have attempted to assess the quality of children's reading interests. The efforts have been expended primarily toward ascertaining quantity or type. Although the problem of determining some measure of quality is much less easily solved than are those related to sheer numbers or categories, efforts in this direction would appear to be highly important in building toward an understanding of how tastes are developed.

There are other techniques used that have not been identified or discussed here. Several approaches developed by investigators working with adult reading interests might well offer appropriate techniques for use with children. In some instances, the rigor of the methodology used by these investigators has surpassed that of most researchers delving into children's reading interests. Strang (1942), for example, combined a case-study approach with larger samples in her effort to get at reading interests of older students and adults. The sampling procedures and techniques used by Waples, Berelson, and Bradshaw (1940) and by Waples and Tyler (1931) need close scrutiny for adaptation to the study of children. We have yet to see an extremely rigorous, exhaustive study in the area of children's reading interests.

In general, the research into children's reading interests has suffered from, among other things, lack of clear definitions and lack of rigor in design, as well as from questionable data-gathering instruments. The instruments appear, for the most part, not to have been scrutinized for reliability or validity, except in the most superficial manner. Through the years the techniques that have been developed seem to have become established by repetition rather than by any careful consideration of their merits or shortcomings. Although there are bright spots, they are infrequent rather than the rule.

RESEARCH IN EYE MOVEMENTS

Interest in eye-movement research may well have reached a peak with the appearance of the National Conference on Visual Information Processing report by the National Institute of Education (1975). A major aspect of that report is the identification of directions for future research. It is quite likely that the report will stimulate a considerable amount of research using eye movements and that large gaps in our knowledge of the reading process may be filled by the research growing out of the suggestions from this conference.

One of the earliest reported research reports on eye movements in reading appears to have been Javal's (1879). His technique was direct observation, which revealed that the eyes move along a line in a series of jerky movements, or saccades, with a pause approximately at every tenth letter. Javal concluded that the eye could take in approximately that amount in each fixation. Other early investigators using the same method concluded that 1.55 words can be read per fixation (Huey 1908).

Huey noted that attempts to count eye movements were made by attaching a microphone to the eyelid and by fastening a small bristle pointer to an ivory cup attached to the cornea, which enabled a tracing to be made by the movements of the eye while reading. Both of these methods were unsuccessful.

Somewhat later, mirrors were used to observe the movements of the eye during reading (Erdmann and Dodge 1898). The investigator could note eye movements while standing behind the subject, who sat in front (and to the left) of a mirror. Erdmann and Dodge found that individual readers tended to be relatively consistent in the number of fixation pauses made from line to line and that fewer fixations were made when the reading material was familiar. These same investigators also used a telescope to observe eye movements. In addition, they used readers' reports of afterimages in the attempt to determine fixation pauses. Readers viewed a brightly illuminated, wedge-shaped piece of red paper until the retina was fatigued. Then, when a passage was read, a green afterimage appeared at the point of each fixation and was reported by the reader.

Huey (1908) followed up on the earlier, unsuccessful efforts to record eye movements by a means more accurate than observation. He made a plaster-of-paris cup molded to fit the cornea. A lever connected the cup to an aluminum pointer that traced on a smoked drum a record of the eye's movements. He noted that, when asked to read rapidly, his subjects decreased both the number and the duration of pauses per line.

Judd, McAllister, and Steele (1905) used a photographic method to record eye movements. A series of photographs were taken of subjects who had a small white flake attached to their corneas. The investigators then determined the eye movements by superimposing on the reading material the positions of the white spots as recorded on the film. Other photographic techniques using film for plates soon followed, and the technique first suggested by Dodge and Cline (1901) and modified in various ways by others is essentially the one still followed. The basic principle is that light is reflected from the cornea onto a film plate of some sort. A thorough description of various devices for accomplishing this may be found in Young and Sheena (1975). Quite recently, a computer technique was developed (McConkie and Rayner 1973) that uses corneal reflection methods. In these corneal reflection methods, the reader's head must be immobilized.

In the early 1920s, the electrooculography technique was developed for measuring the eye's position. It involved placing electrodes on the skin around the eye. According to Young and Sheena (1975), recent advances in this approach have made the electrodes easier to apply and of minimal discomfort. Yet another technique involves tracking limbus, pupil, and eyelid by scanning the eye with a television camera, using infrared illumination.

The various recently used techniques are compared by Young and Sheena (1975) in terms of selected criteria. Most require that the subject not wear glasses or contact lenses; most require, for any degree of accuracy, a great deal of cooperation on the part of the subject; several involve a high degree of subject discomfort; and, in almost all, the subject is well aware of the apparatus. One or two techniques are relatively inexpensive and do not need quite as much head restraint as have earlier techniques.

Reliability studies of eye-movement patterns present mixed results. Apparently, eye-movement records show relatively low reliability for short excerpts, but larger reliability figures may be obtained when longer selections, of twenty to forty lines, are read (Tinker 1936).

Questions must be raised about the validity of eye-movement records obtained in situations in which the subject's head must be immobilized or in which the encroachment of the apparatus is so obvious as to distract the subject from a normal reading attitude. Tinker (1965) reported that subjects who were given opportunities to adapt to the laboratory setting did not show problems in adjusting to the situation. This stand, however, has been questioned.

Most recently, Monty (1975) reported on a system for monitoring eye movements which appears to be both unobtrusive and promising. The system, the EG & G/HEL oculometer, incorporates automatic high-speed processing of the eye movements and minimal constraints on the subject. Indeed, the only constraint imposed is that the subject remain seated in an armchair. The subject's environment is a small room in which she or he is presented with reading material on a small screen approximately one meter on a side. Eye movements are tracked automatically by means of a concealed television camera. Data are fed into a computer and can be recorded on videotape simultaneously. Information concerning such factors as the pattern of eye-movement fixations is provided on a visual display as the subject reads and can be produced as hard copy. At present, the system does not perform well with individuals who wear glasses or with subjects who have low-contrast pupils. However, it is felt that these problems can be solved. Other advantages of the system are that it can provide output on a variety of measures, including such behaviors as changes in pupil size, number of blinks, and average duration of fixations. It is possible to go from monitoring a single subject's eye movements to statistical analysis of group data. No published reports of research using this system have been identified, but the advantages of such a system are obvious. It is possible that eye-movement research previously done with restraining and highly obtrusive instruments can be redone and the findings checked for accuracy.

A considerable body of literature is to be found, covering all aspects of eye movements in reading. It is interesting that the findings from most of the very earliest research remain relatively accurate and have been verified by more recent information. Data have been collected about location, duration, and frequency of fixation, speed of saccadic movements, patterns of pause duration, the role of regressions, and patterns of eye movements during reading of materials of various kinds and levels of difficulty. All of these areas have afforded worthwhile information. However, peculiar to eye-movement research is the opportunity to probe into the reading process in a manner not possible with any other research technique. Although other means have been used to obtain insights into the process, eye-movement research appears to offer unique data about what is happening as individuals read. Eye-movement patterns may represent, in essence, reflections of the thought processes of individuals as they read; at least they are often interpreted as such.

Techniques of collecting data about eye movements reflect the increased use of technology. As better and more sophisticated tools have become available, we have had the opportunity to use them. There are still drawbacks to most of the apparatus which is currently available. With advances in our technological skills, the development of simpler, less constraining methods of recording eye movements will continue.

EYE MOVEMENTS AND READING INTERESTS: SOME CONTRASTS

The two areas briefly highlighted in this chapter have been actively researched for about a century now. A historical view of each points up various techniques that have been used over time. In each area, it is possible to identify a unique pattern of development which is in sharp contrast with the other.

Eye-movement research has been strongly influenced by technological developments. Except in the analysis of data by computer, technology has not had a similar effect on the research tools and techniques used to study reading interests. Of course, the two areas are investigating quite different aspects of the reading field, and although technological developments have aided, limited, and influenced the direction of eye movement research, such developments are not particularly useful to the study of reading interests.

Certain data in eye-movement research tend to be more precise than those collected in investigations of children's reading interests because the techniques and tools of measurement are more precise. Definitions follow a similar pattern. Both definitions and measuring instruments in reading-interest research are suspect because of their vagueness and lack of consistency. Indeed, researchers have talked past one another rather than to one another. In contrast, because the behavior measured is directly observable and is ascertained by highly reliable instruments, definitions and certain measurements in eye-movement research have been far more precise. However, the apparatus used for collecting data have been so obtrusive as to raise questions concerning whether or not a normal reading situation is reflected. In eye-movement research, techniques have been dictated to some extent by available technology; in reading-interest research, little creative, rigorous effort has been made toward developing finer techniques. Rather, research techniques have tended to follow earlier research patterns, and the development of instrumentation has not progressed much beyond a horse-and-buggy stage.

Rationale and conceptual framework constitute another source of sharp distinction. Generally, research into children's reading interests is based on an immediate, practical rationale. Little effort has been expended to establish a theoretical base in the psychology of motivation, interest, need, and drive. Eye-movement research, however, does tend to build a theoretical framework. Such a framework goes back at least to Huey (1908), who developed a theoretical rationale in perception, as well as in the thinking process.

The differences in source of rationale and in theoretical base can, in part, be traced to the backgrounds of the individuals involved in the research. Investigations into eye movements have generally been carried out by psychologists doing basic research; research into children's reading interests has tended to be done by educators or by those with a distinct classroom orientation and a need to solve immediate practical problems. Both areas are important. Each, by its nature, has attracted a different type of researcher, and, as a result, each field of research has quite a different orientation.

CONCLUSION

In this chapter, an attempt has been made to spotlight the historical development of research in two distinct areas of reading. The direction of study and the development of research techniques and tools in each have been highlighted. An attempt has not been made to synthesize the research findings but rather to point out the development of research methods and to contrast certain aspects of these methods. In each area, the future holds more promise than the past.

REFERENCES

Dodge, Raymond, and Cline, C. T. "The Angle Velocity of Eye Movements." *Psychological Review* 8 (March 1901): 145—57.

Erdmann, B., and Dodge, R. *Psychologische Untersuchungen über das Lesen, auf Experimeuteller Grundlage.* Halle: Max Niemyer, 1898.

Huey, Edmund B. *The Psychology and Pedagogy of Reading.* New York: Macmillan Co., 1908.

Javal, Emile. "Essai sur la physiologie de la lecture." *Annales D'Oculistique* 82 (1879): 242—53.

Judd, Charles H.; McAllister, C. N.; and Steele, W. M. "General Introduction to a Series of Studies of Eye-Movements by Means of Kinetoscopic Photographs." *Psychological Review Monograph Supplements* 7 (1905): 1—16.

McConkie, G. W., and Rayner, K. "The Span of the Effective Stimulus during Fixations in Reading." Paper presented at the meeting of the American Educational Research Association, 1973. [ED 083 579]

Monty, R. A. "An Advanced Eye-Movement Measuring and Recording System." *American Psychologist* 30 (March 1975): 331—35.

National Institute of Education. *National Conference on Visual Information Processing.* Washington, D.C.: U.S. Department of Health, Education, and Welfare, 1975.

Norvell, G. W. *The Reading Interests of Young People.* Boston: D. C. Heath and Co., 1950.

Robinson, Helen M., and Weintraub, Sam. "Research Related to Children's Interests and to Developmental Values of Reading." *Library Trends* 22 (October 1973): 81—108.

Stanchfield, J. M. "Boys' Reading Interests as Revealed through Personal Conferences." *Reading Teacher* 16 (September 1962): 41—44.

Strang, Ruth. *Exploration in Reading Patterns.* Chicago: University of Chicago Press, 1942.

Terman, L. M., and Lima, M. *Children's Reading.* New York: Appleton-Century Co., 1925.

Tinker, Miles A. "Reliability and Validity of Eye-Movement Measures of Reading." *Journal of Experimental Psychology* 19 (December 1936): 732—46.

——. *Bases for Effective Reading.* Minneapolis: University of Minnesota Press, 1965.

True, M. B. C. "What My Pupils Read." *Education* 10 (1889): 42—45.

Waples, D., and Tyler, R. W. *What People Want to Read About: A Study of Group Interests and a Survey of Problems in Adult Reading.* Chicago: American Library Association and the University of Chicago Press, 1931.

Waples, D.; Berelson, B.; and Bradshaw, F. R. *What Reading Does to People.* Chicago: University of Chicago Press, 1940.

Wragg, Marie. "The Leisure Activities of Boys and Girls." *Educational Research* 10 (February 1968): 139—44.

Young, L. R., and Sheena, D. "Eye-Movement Measurement Techniques." *American Psychologist* 30 (March 1975): 316—30.

The Roots of
Reading Diagnosis

PETER L. PELOSI
State University of New York at Buffalo

In this chapter, a doctoral candidate presents a succinct overview of the origins of reading diagnosis in the United States and traces the development of the concept from its infancy in 1896 through the next fifty years. He begins with definitions, proceeds to the development of the concept, highlights the contributions of the "scientific movement" in education, and finally illustrates the kinds of guidelines for diagnosis that grew out of classic studies.

DEFINITIONS

The term *reading diagnosis* has undergone minor changes in meaning as the procedure has been more and more refined. Many different definitions and conceptualizations of reading diagnosis appear in the literature. Each researcher has defined the term or outlined the concept with respect to the approach used in a specific study. In general, three different concepts of reading diagnosis seem to have developed over the years, each having a slightly different view of diagnosis. These three major concepts, or types, might be classified remedial, causative, and research oriented.

An example of the remedial concept was C. T. Gray's (1922) definition of reading diagnosis as "that procedure which enables the teacher to determine the difficulties of those pupils who are below standards for their grade level" (p. 7). Gray's use of the word "procedure" within the definition allowed him to present in his book, *Deficiencies in Reading Ability*, what he believed to be a comprehensive method for studying individuals in order to improve methods of reading instruction.

Monroe (1932), in an example of the causative type of reading diagnosis, advanced a multiple-causation approach for determining reading disability. Her implicit definition of reading diagnosis required the acquisition of information in a number of areas that may contribute to reading disability. In Monroe's approach, the main concern of a reading diagnosis was to investigate, by formal methods, that constellation of factors inhibiting a child's ability to learn to read. Strang (1940) extended this concept of reading diagnosis to include a detailed description of the reading difficulties deterring an individual's progress in reading. She also outlined a procedure which would enable the diagnostician to establish reasons for a student's failure in reading. Robinson (1946) further extended and refined the multiple-causation theory by involving a group of specialists in the diagnosis of retarded readers. She did not explicitly state a definition of reading diagnosis but outlined a procedure for determining the factors that cause reading retardation.

The third type of reading diagnosis is research oriented and has its basis in the investigation of the reading process. Reading diagnosis as a research base was used as an educational tool for the examination of select aspects of the reading process. C. T. Gray (1917), Judd and Buswell (1922), Dearborn (1930), and Spache (1943) illustrated the value of elements of reading diagnosis as a means for critically studying the act of reading. The use of diagnosis and the refinement of specific aspects of it not only aided in expanding knowledge of the process but also pointed to the need for more critical definition of the elements involved in reading diagnosis.

DEVELOPMENT OF THE CONCEPT OF DIAGNOSIS

Failure to learn to read is not a twentieth-century discovery or phenomenon. Both reading failure and the attempt to remedy the problem have been reported by historians, philosophers, and statesmen, as early as the beginning of the seventeenth century. Mathews (1966) reported, in his history of reading instruction, early accounts of individuals experiencing reading difficulties in England, Germany, and colonial America. Both Smith (1965) and Hyatt (1943), in their historical treatments of reading, indicated early awareness of what today is recognized as reading disability. However, even by the twentieth century there was little information available to educators for the diagnosis of reading problems, although those problems were apparent. Reading difficulties existed, but the techniques necessary for their diagnosis were, at the turn of the century, in their infancy. The development of reading diagnosis began then. The causes for the growth of reading diagnosis and its development from the beginning of the twentieth century are the subject of this historical investigation.

A number of sociocultural factors gave impetus to the burgeoning interest in reading as education in the U.S. entered the twentieth century. Among these factors was the acceleration of technological progress; such development created a demand for a more highly educated citizenry within the social, political, and economic strata of society. Educational institutions began to have a more involved commitment to both the student and the community. Education needed to meet societal demands by complementing and supplementing technological expansion. The need for an educational counterpart to societal development resulted in the example set by the compulsory attendance laws. Compulsory school attendance, consummated by the 1920s, was an attempt by government to effect mass education. Equal education for all became a must; the demand for literacy encouraged the formulation of new goals for an institution's educational obligation to its community. In turn, the demand for a literate society has generated widening interest in our schools and their educational programs. This increased interest has helped pave the way for new areas in education.

Another factor leading to the development of reading diagnosis was the recognition of reading disability as an educational problem. Rice (1897) spearheaded the movement for examining and evaluating educational problems, and a turning point for reading disability may well have been the publication of "A Case of Congenital Word Blindness" by Morgan (1896). Morgan described, and attempted to determine the cause of, an individual's failure to make normal progress in learning to read. Morgan's work helped to focus educational attention upon classifying causes for reading problems by examining the reading process (Quantz 1897). These investigations of the process of reading pointed to yet another factor that seems to have contributed to the development of reading diagnosis. Studies were conducted with disabled readers, as means of examining and defining the normal reading process; these were part of a growing movement toward more precise investigations of reading (Huey 1901; Dearborn 1906). Knowledge gained by educational research contributed a great deal to the development of reading diagnosis.

THE SCIENTIFIC MOVEMENT

Concurrent with the publication of Morgan's study, the scientific movement in education continued to grow; the foundations of this movement were built upon the work of Galton, Binet, Cattell, and Thorndike. It was Rice, however, who brought to the attention of educators the importance of applying research methods to educational problems. Of extreme importance to the scientific movement, and an integral part of it, was the development of educational measurement. The development and refinement of educational measurement techniques greatly contributed to the emergence of interest in problems associated with learning to read. Measurement became an important factor contributing to the eventual development of reading diagnosis.

It seems, from a historical perspective, that the recognition of the importance of reading to society, the failure of many to learn to read, the movement to scientifically investigate existing educational problems, and the development of measurement instruments for education, all aided early researchers in developing procedures for diagnosing reading problems. By approximately 1915, the educational-measurement movement was viewed by many educationists as a viable means to evaluate the products of instruction. Thorndike (1914), for example, developed the first normed reading-measurement scale for educational use. W. S. Gray (1914, 1917) followed by constructing a tentative scale for the measurement of oral reading ability. This scale was extended, refined, and adapted by experimental and scientific techniques and, at the time, was accepted as a reliable and valid measurement of a student's ability to read orally.

As instruments were developed and used for the measurement of reading ability, it became more evident to educators that a significant number of students either were failing to learn to read or were performing far below expected levels (Wallin 1922). Because of the development of measurement instruments, the investigations of reading disabilities could be objectively studied. Uhl (1916) appears to be the first to have used reading tests as a means to identify classroom reading problems. He introduced a procedure for the diagnosis of reading defects by the use of three different reading tests and clinical observations of students. Uhl's study was followed by the research of C. T. Gray (1917), Zirbes (1918), Freeman (1920), W. S. Gray (1921), and others. The thrust of these investigations was the establishment of procedures for diagnosing reading disability; they also provided a framework for later studies investigating causes for reading disability.

GUIDELINES FOR DIAGNOSIS

The importance of the diagnosis of reading problems was further highlighted by the research of W. S. Gray (1922), Horn (1923), and Merton (1923). Their publications are historically linked, as they not only emphasized the value of diagnosis but also offered diagnostic formats and methodologies and descriptions of children failing to learn to read. Additional emphasis was placed on the importance of diagnosis by the presentation of specific case studies demonstrating the usefulness, practicality, and logic of developing a more precise diagnostic technique for investigating reading disability. For example, Anderson and Merton (1920, 1921) used the results of diagnosis as a method for planning instruction. In the same vein, Geiger (1923) presented results of a reading diagnosis and wrote of the value of these results in planning remedial work. Although the direction of those studies was basically for planning remedial programs, reading diagnosis as an educational tool helped make remediation possible.

During the early 1920s, a general interest began to develop in reading diagnosis as an aid to educational progress; this emerging interest aided in the development of more specific guidelines for conducting diagnoses. C. T. Gray (1922) wrote the first professional book to deal specifically with conducting a reading diagnosis and understanding the concepts involved. Woolley and Ferris (1923) conducted a longitudinal study of specific case studies in reading; each case study was based upon a structured diagnosis. However, despite C. T. Gray's and Woolley and Ferris's attempts to establish guidelines for conducting diagnoses, there was yet a general lack of information regarding what one needed to ascertain when diagnosing individual students. Assistance soon followed, however, with suggestions by Horn (1923), Ford (1924), and Zirbes (1925), who reported clear and specific techniques.

Concurrent with the growth and development of the beginning stages of reading diagnosis was the expansion of research about the reading process. The works of Quantz (1897), Huey (1901, 1908), and Dearborn (1906) provided a basic foundation for the research that was to follow. By the early part of the 1920s, there was serious experimentation with the nature of the reading process that helped establish awareness of possible difficulties connected with learning to read. Buswell (1920, 1921, 1922) conducted several such studies which, along with the efforts of others, served as a basis for the conceptualization of factors to be examined in a reading diagnosis. The growth in reading diagnosis was further enhanced by studies undertaken to investigate specific causes for failure in learning to read and to refine diagnostic techniques (Monroe 1932; Betts 1934; Gates 1935; Tinker 1938; Strang 1940; Robinson 1946).

The first half of the twentieth century appears to have provided much guidance for the present. Although there is presently a good deal of money, time, and energy spent in the area of diagnosing an individual's reading ability, there appears to be no single source which laid the historical foundations for such an allocation of resources. There is no synthesis of the periods of growth, inactivity, or controversy in the development of reading diagnosis. This writer is now at work on such a focus, which should further tie research and authoritative opinion together to enhance our knowledge concerning diagnostic procedures and practices.

REFERENCES

Anderson, C. J., and Merton, Elda. "Remedial Work in Reading." *Elementary School Journal* 20 (May 1920): 685—701; (June 1920): 772—91.
———. "Remedial Work in Silent Reading." *Elementary School Journal* 21 (January 1921): 336—48.
Betts, Emmett Albert. "Teacher Analysis of Reading Disabilities." *Elementary English Review* 11 (April 1934): 99—102.
Buswell, Guy Thomas. *An Experimental Study of the Eye Voice Span in Reading.* Supplementary Educational Monographs, no. 17. Chicago: Department of Education, University of Chicago, 1920.
———. "The Relationship between Eye-Perceptions and Voice Response in Reading." *Journal of Educational Psychology* 12 (April 1921): 217—27.
———. *Fundamental Reading Habits: A Study of Their Development.* Supplementary Educational Monographs, no. 21. Chicago: Department of Education, University of Chicago, 1922.
Dearborn, Walter F. "The Psychology of Reading." *Archives of Psychology,* 1 (March 1906): 71—132.
———. "The Nature of Special Abilities and Disabilities." *School and Society* 31 (May 1930): 623—36.
Ford, F. A. "Diagnostic Supervision." *Journal of the Louisiana Teachers' Association* 1 (April 1924): 30—35.
Freeman, Frank N. "Clinical Study as a Method in Experimental Education." *Journal of Applied Psychology* 4 (June-September 1920): 126—41.

Gates, Arthur I. "Recent Developments in Diagnostic and Remedial Teaching in Reading." In *The Application of Research Findings to Current Educational Practices*, pp. 83—91. Official report of the American Educational Association. Washington, D.C.: National Educational Association, 1935.

――――. "Viewpoints Underlying the Study of Reading Disabilities." *Elementary English Review* 12 (April 1935): 85—90, 105.

Geiger, Ruth. "A Study in Reading Diagnosis." *Journal of Educational Research* 8 (November 1923): 283—300.

Gray, Clarence Truman. *Types of Reading Ability as Exhibited through Tests and Laboratory Experiments.* Supplementary Educational Monographs, vol. 1, no. 5. Chicago: Department of Education, University of Chicago, 1917.

――――. *Deficiencies in Reading Ability: Their Diagnosis and Remedies.* Boston: D. C. Heath and Co., 1922.

Gray, William S. "A Tentative Scale for the Measurement of Oral Reading Achievement." Master's thesis, Columbia University, 1914.

――――. *Studies of Elementary School Reading through Standardized Tests.* Supplementary Educational Monographs, vol. 1, no. 1. Chicago: Department of Education, University of Chicago, 1917.

――――. "Diagnostic and Remedial Steps in Reading." *Journal of Educational Research* 4 (June 1921): 1—15.

Gray, William S., and others. *Remedial Cases in Reading: Their Diagnosis and Treatment.* Supplementary Educational Monographs, no. 22. Chicago: Department of Education, University of Chicago, 1922.

Horn, Ernest. "The Objectives in Reading as a Guide to Remedial and Prophylactic Work." In *The Problem of the Elementary School Principal in Light of the Testing Movement*, pp. 287—96. Washington, D.C.: Department of Elementary School Principals of the National Education Association, 1923.

Huey, Edmund Burke. "On the Psychology and Physiology of Reading." *American Journal of Psychology* 12 (April 1901): 292—313.

――――. *The Psychology and Pedagogy of Reading.* New York: MacMillan Co., 1908.

Hyatt, Ada V. *The Place of Oral Reading in the School Program: Its History and Development from 1880 to 1941.* Contributions to Education, no. 872. New York: Teachers College, Columbia University, 1943.

Judd, Charles Hubbard, and Buswell, G. T. *Silent Reading: A Study of the Various Types.* Supplementary Educational Monographs, no. 23. Chicago: Department of Education, University of Chicago, 1922.

Mathews, Mitford M. *Teaching to Read: Historically Considered.* Chicago: University of Chicago Press, 1966. [ED 117 649]

Merton, Elda. "The Discovery and Correction of Reading Difficulties." In *The Problem of the Elementary School Principal in Light of the Testing Movement*, pp. 346—63. Washington, D.C.: Department of Elementary School Principals of the National Education Association, 1923.

Monroe, Marion. "Methods for Diagnosis and Treatment for Cases of Reading Disability." *Genetic Psychology Monographs* 4 (October-November 1928): 335—456.

――――. *Diagnostic Reading Examination: Manual of Directions.* Chicago: C. H. Stoelling Co., 1931.

――――. *Children Who Cannot Read.* Chicago: University of Chicago Press, 1932.

Morgan, W. P. "A Case of Congenital Word Blindness." *British Medical Journal*, 2 (November 1896): 1612.

Orton, S. T. *Reading, Writing and Speech Problems in Children: A Presentation of Certain Types of Disorders in the Development of Language Faculty.* New York: W. W. Norton, 1937.

Quantz, J. O. "Problems in the Psychology of Reading." *Psychological Review Monograph Supplements* 2 (1897).

Robinson, Helen M. *Why Pupils Fail in Reading.* Chicago: University of Chicago Press, 1946.

Rice, Joseph Mayer. "The Futility of the Spelling Grind." *The Forum* 23. (April 1897): 163—72; (June 1897): 409—19.

Smith, Nila Banton. *American Reading Instruction.* Newark, Delaware: International Reading Association, 1965.

Spache, George. "Eye Preference, Visual Acuity and Reading Ability." *Elementary School Journal* 43 (May 1943): 539—43.

Strang, Ruth. "Diagnosis and Remediation." In *Reading in General Education.* Washington, D.C.: American Council on Education, 1940.

Thorndike, E. L. "The Measurement of Ability in Reading." *Teachers College Record* 15 (September 1914): 207—27.

Tinker, Miles A. "Trends in Diagnostic and Remedial Reading Shown by Recent Publications in the Field." *Journal of Educational Research,* 32 (December 1938): 293—303.

Uhl, Willis L. "The Use of the Results of Reading Tests as Bases for Planning Remedial Work." *Elementary School Journal* 17 (December 1916): 266—75.

Wallin, J. E. Wallace. *The Achievement of Subnormal Children in Standardized Educational Tests.* Miami University Bulletin, series no. 7. Oxford, Ohio: Miami University, 1922.

Woolley, Helen Thompson, and Ferris, Elizabeth. *Diagnosis and Treatment of Young School Failures.* Bureau of Education Bulletin, no. 1. Washington, D.C.: United States Bureau of Education, 1923.

Zirbes, Laura. "Diagnostic Measurement as a Basis for Procedure." *Elementary School Journal* 18 (March 1918): 505—12.

———. "Attacking the Causes of Reading Deficiency." *Teachers College Record* 26 (June 1925): 956—66.

Remedial Reading in Secondary Schools: Three-Fourths of a Century

WILLIAM P. COWAN
Hofstra University

In this chapter, a doctoral candidate develops a brief but comprehensive historical picture of remedial reading instruction in American secondary schools from 1900 through the present. He begins by stating the delimitations of a historical view of remedial reading in secondary schools, discusses early efforts, traces the wide spread of remedial reading instruction from World War II on, and emphasizes the role of funding in carrying on such programs.

DELIMITATIONS

The delimitations of a historical investigation of remedial reading have been clearly established for the elementary level by Pangalangan (1960) and Anderson (1968) and for the secondary level by Schleich (1967) and Hill (1971). Anderson stated that "the majority of the work in remedial reading has been done in this century; in fact, there was no known work in remedial reading prior to 1900" (p. 3). Schleich said that "a review of the literature shows a dearth of published remedial reading research studies at the secondary level" (p. 109), while Hill found

> little specific attention has been given to the emergence and development of secondary reading programs. The earliest professional society publications to treat secondary reading tended to subsume reading as a function of general teacher activity. The usual historical sources on reading give the secondary reading program but brief attention. (P. 20)

No distinction has been made in this chapter between corrective and remedial reading, even though some authorities have drawn a line of demarcation. The definition of remedial reading selected for this study was found in Good's (1973) *Dictionary of Education:* in reading instruction, activities planned for individuals or for groups of pupils in order to provide for both the diagnosis of reading difficulties and their correction (p. 475).

THE BEGINNINGS

Although secondary-school-age individuals with reading disabilities were studied by ophthalmologists and psychologists as far back as the latter part of the nineteenth century and the early part of the twentieth century, secondary school remedial reading programs did not develop until after World War I. Their development was a direct result of public awareness of the illiteracy of large numbers of members of the armed forces, who were unable to function effectively in the service because of their inability to read. Hill (1971) suggested that, "after the war, changing technological patterns, the occupational difficulties of the Great Depression, [and] a growing sophistication among the citizenry . . . reinforced public and professional awareness of the value of a secondary education as well as for adequacy in reading skill" (p. 22).

Iowa University's Bureau of Educational Research in 1929 administered the Iowa High School Silent Reading Tests to seven thousand junior and senior high school students throughout the state. The results of the testing program were analyzed and interpreted to determine the wide range of silent reading abilities and disabilities. The bureau then published a bulletin based upon the results of the testing program, which made specific suggestions to teachers for the administration of a program to correct the identified defects. The bulletin was entitled *A Remedial Program for Silent Reading in the High School* (Greene 1930).

The first large-scale remedial reading program in a public school system was begun in New York City during the depression of the mid-1930s and lasted until World War II. The secondary schools were involved, and the program was described by Center and Bersons (1937) in their book *Teaching High-School Students to Read: A Study of Retardation in Reading.* Another outstanding book, by McCallister (1936), published one year earlier, focused on remedial procedures for specific reading deficiencies noted by the author as he observed high school students at work. The volume appeared to be the first attempt to apply the results of research immediately at the secondary school level.

WORLD WAR II AND AFTERMATH

Blair (1941) conducted a national survey of remedial teaching in senior high schools; he contacted over one thousand high school principals in cities with populations of twenty thousand or more. Responses were received from 379 principals in thirty-eight states and the District of Columbia. Over fifty percent of the schools provided special sections of

English or remedial reading classes for poor readers; twenty percent did little or nothing. In ten percent of the cases, the responsibility was carried by English teachers in regular classes; in about seven percent, a specialist was provided who coached individuals or small groups; and, in about seven percent, the responsibility was assumed, according to the survey, by all teachers.

In 1942 the National Education Association issued a research bulletin based on a survey of 2,275 high schools. Half of the schools claimed they were "doing something" for the most seriously retarded readers; about forty percent stated that "some" attention was also given to the less seriously handicapped. Ten percent reported no systematic aid was given the retarded reader. Almost fifty percent of the principals who responded said that reading was one of the school's most acute instructional problems. According to the teachers who participated in the survey, the development of readiness to read the materials appropriate to the student's age and grade level was the major step needed to improve comprehension.

During the war years (1941—1946), output of reading research and instructional materials diminished greatly, teacher-training programs were curtailed, and there was a teacher shortage at the secondary level. However, the public and the professionals became aware of the literacy levels of draftees for World War II and were aroused once again. The military developed special training units to give illiterate and non-English-speaking personnel academic training. They applied tested and established remedial methods and succeeded in developing an amazingly efficient program, one that enabled the average illiterate to acquire, in eight weeks, the basic academic skills needed for military life. The realization that reading could be taught to these young people in army camps in an amazingly short time led to an increase in secondary remedial programs after the war, when it was discovered that there were reading deficiencies in large numbers of high school and college students. The GI Bill provided the means for former teachers to take graduate degrees; many of them began teaching at the secondary level better equipped to teach reading. Universities began offering courses dealing with secondary reading. The National Society for the Study of Education (NSSE) published a yearbook (1948) that focused on reading in high school and college.

Witty and Brink (1949) received questionnaire responses from 109 secondary schools of 500 contacted about remedial reading practices. Eighty-nine percent replied that the responsibility for remedial reading instruction was assumed by the English department. Twenty-one percent emphasized the improvement of students' ability to read and to study the materials in other content areas. Students selected for remedial work were chosen by supervisors, administrators, or teachers, on the basis of standardized test scores. The investigators stated:

> Of the one hundred twenty-six teachers who were reported
> to be teaching remedial reading courses only twenty-eight were

full time specialists. The other ninety-eight were regular teachers who volunteered or were drafted for the work. A majority of them had no special preparation for the work. Seventy-five schools used the same teachers as long as the program had been in operation. Twenty-one schools passed the classes around. (P. 203)

Smith (1965) indicated that, until 1948, the year in which the NSSE's yearbook *Reading in the High School and College* appeared, any reading instruction that had been done at the higher levels was remedial in nature. Gray suggested a sound reading program for high schools and colleges, in addition to remedial instruction. Bond and Bond, in their book entitled *Developmental Reading in High School* (1941), first used the term "developmental reading" to distinguish a program planned in terms of the development of all high school students from a remedial program for special students (p. 296).

Hill (1971) tended to support the idea that remedial reading dominated the secondary area in the late forties and early fifties. He stated, "The remedial reading class or program was one of the most common secondary types," which he thought was not surprising in view of the fact that many teachers and school officers still believed that reading was an elementary-school subject. He argued further that "the simultaneous emergence of the concepts of secondary reading, remedial reading, and the reading specialist in professional training programs during that period tended to homogenize their images" (p. 24).

The apparent fear of the spread of communism seemed to stimulate remedial instruction at all levels in the United States, twice during the fifties. In 1950, after the Communists had attacked the Republic of Korea, President Truman declared a national emergency, to strengthen the United States. The concern for national preservation caused changes to be made in materials that children had to read in school, particularly in social studies and science. Teaching reading in the content fields became tremendously important. The second challenge came with Sputnik in 1957 and with the development of Soviet nuclear armaments. The technological supremacy of the United States was now challenged by the achievement of the Soviet Union, which vowed to establish world communism. Government grants were poured into the educational system to improve reading at all levels.

FUNDING

The growth of remedial and corrective programs at the secondary level in the sixties and early seventies accelerated dramatically. This can be traced directly to millions of dollars in federal grants provided by the National Defense Education Act (NDEA), which helped train reading personnel through special training institutes; this act stimulated the growth of courses in remedial reading at the secondary level at almost two hundred universities. The Elementary and Secondary Education Act (ESEA) of

1965 provided hundreds of millions of dollars for new programs for the retraining of the jobless, poverty-stricken, and culturally disadvantaged. The public and the government during this period recognized the remedial reading program as a service essential to obtaining societal goals.

The success of the NDEA and ESEA programs was reflected in a statement made by Thomas K. Glennan, Jr., (1974) in his role as director of the National Institute of Education (NIE). Speaking before the House of Representatives Appropriations Committee, he said:

> The American Education System continues to prepare millions of persons for productive and happy lives in our society. The percent of eighteen year olds graduating from high schools has increased from sixty-seven percent in 1960 to about eighty percent; the proportions graduating from college has increased seventeen percent in 1960 of those of graduate age to more than twenty-three percent. The illiteracy had declined to a point that roughly one percent of those fourteen or older cannot read or write a simple message, less than half those in the same category in 1959. The American people, quite correctly perceive education as a key to their future well-being. (P. 787)

Dr. Muikhead, speaking before the same committee, reported that: "In the time the public library programs have been supported, from 1956 to 1974, more than six hundred million in federal support has been more than matched by State and local efforts. We have now reached the point where library services are available for ninety-four percent of the people" (p. 232).

CONCLUSION

Glennan and Muikhead's reports indicated that progress has been made in reducing illiteracy in the United States, in promoting higher levels of educational attainment, and in expanding library facilities. There has been growth in secondary reading programs, both developmental and remedial, in variety and in number. However, there has been no real attempt to assess the quality of these programs. Hill's conclusion remains accurate: "We know very little more about secondary reading instruction and program operation . . . than we did one or two decades ago because, with few exceptions, program surveys have failed to provide detailed and carefully defined results" (1970, p. 28).

This writer is involved in a nationwide survey to assess secondary remedial instruction in the United States, as part of this effort to determine major trends and developments in secondary remedial reading instruction since 1900. One expectation of the survey is that the findings will help gauge what is being done in secondary remedial reading instruction and, by inference, will indicate what further studies and procedures should be seriously considered for the future.

REFERENCES

Anderson, William James. "A Study of the Evolution of Remedial Reading in the Elementary Schools of America, 1900—1964." Doctoral dissertation, Baylor University, 1968.

Blair, Glenn Myers. "Remedial Reading Programs in Senior High Schools." *School Review* 49 (January 1941): 32—41.

Bond, Guy, and Bond, Eva. *Developmental Reading in High School.* New York: MacMillan Co., 1941.

Center, Stella S., and Persons, Gladys L. *Teaching High School Students to Read.* National Council of Teachers of English, English Monographs, no. 6. New York: D. Appleton-Century Co., 1937.

Glennan, Thomas K., Jr. *Testimony of Thomas K. Glennan, Jr., Director, National Institute of Education before the Labor-Health, Education, and Welfare Subcommittee of the House Committee on Appropriations in Support of an FY 1974 Supplemental Appropriation.*

Good, Carter V., ed. *Dictionary of Education.* 2nd ed. New York: McGraw-Hill Co., 1959.

Greene, Harry Andrew. *A Remedial Program for Silent Reading in the High School.* University of Iowa Extension Bulletin, no. 240. Iowa City: University of Iowa, 1930.

Hill, Walter. "Characteristics of Secondary Reading: 1940—1970." In *Reading: The Right to Participate*, edited by Frank P. Greene, pp. 20—29. Yearbook of the National Reading Conference, 1971. [ED 049 887]

McCallister, James M. *Remedial and Corrective Instruction in Reading.* New York: D. Appleton-Century Co., 1936.

National Education Association, Research Division. "Reading Instruction in Secondary Schools." *Research Bulletin of the National Education Association* 20 (January 1942).

National Society for the Study of Education, Committee on Reading. *Reading in the High School and College.* Chicago: University of Chicago Press, 1948.

Pangalangan, Vicenta Pacheco. "A History of Remedial Reading Instruction in Elementary Schools in the United States." Doctoral dissertation, Northwestern University, 1960.

Schleich, Miriam. "Remedial Studies at the Secondary Level." In *Combining Research Results and Good Practice*, edited by M. A. Dawson, pp. 109—16. Newark, Delaware: International Reading Association, 1967.

Smith, Nila Banton. *American Reading Instruction.* Newark, Delaware: International Reading Association, 1965.

Witty, Paul, and Brink, William G. "Remedial Reading Practices in the Secondary School." *Journal of Educational Psychology* 40 (April 1949): 193—205.